3rd Edition

Pre-Intermediate

MARKET LEADER

Business English Practice File

John Rogers

Contents

	LANGUAGE WORK			TALK BUSINESS	
	VOCABULARY	**LANGUAGE REVIEW**	**WRITING**	**SOUND WORK**	**SURVIVAL BUSINESS ENGLISH**
UNIT 1 CAREERS *page 4 /page 54*	Words for talking about jobs	Requests Past abilities	Curriculum vitae Applying for a job Editing	**Individual sounds:** The difference between /ɪ/ and /iː/ **Connected speech:** *can /can't* **Stress and intonation:** Questions	Telephoning
UNIT 2 COMPANIES *page 8 /page 56*	Words for talking about companies	Present tenses	Informal e-mails Editing Linking ideas	**Individual sounds:** -*s* endings **Connected speech:** *are*	Company presentations
UNIT 3 SELLING *page 12 /page 58*	Words for talking about selling	Modals	Placing an order Replying to an order Editing	Silent letters **Individual sounds:** Sound–spelling relationships **Connected speech:** *have to*	Negotiating
UNIT 4 GREAT IDEAS *page 16 /page 60*	Verb–noun combinations	Past tenses	Giving information Editing	**Individual sounds:** -*ed* endings **Connected speech:** *was* and *were*	Meetings
UNIT 5 STRESS *page 20 /page 62*	Words for talking about stress in the workplace	The present perfect tense	Punctuation Reports Editing	Groups of consonants **Connected speech:** *has/have; hasn't/haven't* **Stress and intonation:** Question tags	Making and responding to suggestions
UNIT 6 ENTERTAINING *page 24 /page 64*	Words for talking about food and drink	Multiword verbs	Reports Hotel bookings	**Individual sounds:** Sound–spelling relationships **Connected speech:** Weak form of prepositions Consonant–vowel links	Making small talk

THE SOUNDS OF ENGLISH: *page 52*

USING A DICTIONARY: *page 53*

SOUNDS AND SPELLING: *page 53*

		LANGUAGE WORK			TALK BUSINESS	
		VOCABULARY	LANGUAGE REVIEW	WRITING	SOUND WORK	SURVIVAL BUSINESS ENGLISH
UNIT 7 NEW BUSINESS *page 28 /page 66*		Words for talking about the economy	Time clauses	Linking ideas Reports Editing	**Individual sounds:** /ɒ/ and /ɔː/ **Stress and intonation:** Saying the date	Numbers
UNIT 8 MARKETING *page 32/page 68*		Words for talking about marketing	Question formation	Answering enquiries Reports Editing	**Individual sounds:** The letter *a* **Connected speech:** *do you, did you, would you*	Using stress to correct information Getting the message right
UNIT 9 PLANNING *page 36 /page 70*		Words for talking about plans	Talking about the future	Linking ideas Scheduling Editing	**Individual sounds:** The letter *o* **Connected speech:** *to* **Stress and intonation:** Stressed syllables	Meetings Checking information
UNIT 10 MANAGING PEOPLE *page 40 /page 72*		Verbs and prepositions	Reported speech	Reports Requesting information	**Individual sounds:** Matching sounds **Connected speech:** Consonant–vowel links **Stress and intonation:** Stressed syllables	Socialising Taking a message
UNIT 11 CONFLICT *page 44 /page 74*		Words for talking about negotiations	Conditionals	Business letters Editing	**Individual sounds:** The *schwa* sound **Connected speech:** Contractions **Stress and intonation:** Conditional sentences	Dealing with conflict
UNIT 12 PRODUCTS *page 48 /page 76*		Words for talking about products	Passives	Linking ideas Enquiring about a product Editing	Groups of consonants **Connected speech:** *its, it has, it is* **Stress and intonation:** Main stresses	Asking questions about a product Presenting a product

SHADOWING: *page 53*   **ANSWER KEY:** *page 78*   **AUDIO SCRIPTS:** *page 89*

Careers

VOCABULARY **A** Choose the best word (a, b or c) to complete each space in the advert.

Lambrois 303
Your careers guidance service

If you don't have a career .....*path*.....[1] in mind or if you are tired of your old nine-to-five ....[2] and want to make a career ....[3], you can just call us on the telephone number below to find out how we can help you.

We will work with you to understand what is really important to you. For example, are you more interested in ....[4] a lot of money or in having the opportunity to ....[5] the career ladder?

Our experienced counsellors will also review your existing skills, experience and ....[6] to help guide you into a role that will be right for you. They may also ask you to ....[7] a psychometric test to help them to understand what areas of ....[8] suit you best. Maybe you are thinking of a job in finance but are you really good with ....[9]? Or a position in ....[10] resources but do you really enjoy dealing with people and their needs?

Don't delay, call us today on: **020 72489894**.

1	a) ladder	b) path ⟨circled⟩		c) opportunity
2	a) work	b) job		c) employee
3	a) move	b) training		c) break
4	a) doing	b) earning		c) taking
5	a) climb	b) follow		c) earn
6	a) diplomas	b) levels		c) qualifications
7	a) give	b) make		c) do
8	a) employment	b) progress		c) job
9	a) figures	b) counts		c) maths
10	a) personnel	b) staff		c) human

B Complete each sentence with the correct form of an item from the box.

to involve   to be in charge   to deal   to look   to make sure   to be responsible

1 Lev Migachov works in research and development. His job .....*involves*.... developing new products and new ideas.

2 Suzana Lonza is the receptionist. She .... after visitors and takes messages.

3 Nadine Deschamps works for HR. She .... with staff problems, as well as with recruitment and training.

4 Linda Eriksen is our Quality Control Inspector. She .... for monitoring our products and trying to improve their quality.

5 Jose Manzano is our Security Officer. He .... that our staff and premises are protected against crime.

6 Hans Reiter is our new Maintenance Engineer. He checks all our equipment regularly and .... of all repairs.

4

C Complete the phrases from exercise B with the words that come immediately after them.

1 to be in charge ....*of*.........   4 to make sure   ....

2 to deal   ....   5 to be responsible ....

3 to look   ....

LANGUAGE REVIEW

Requests

A Complete the interviewer's questions from a job interview with words from the box.

contact   let   moving   send   sharing   start   ~~working~~

1 Would you mind .....*working*... at weekends?

2 Could you .... us have your previous employer's details?

3 Would you mind .... our appointment to Monday?

4 Could you .... in two weeks' time?

5 Could you .... us as soon as possible?

6 Would you mind .... an office with three other people?

7 Could you .... us a copy of your certificates?

B Match the interviewee's answers to the interviewer's questions in exercise A.

a) Not at all, as long as it's in the morning.   `3`

b) Certainly. I'm free to start as soon as you like.   ☐

c) Yes. I'll let you know my decision by Friday, if that's all right.   ☐

d) Sure. I'll put copies in the post straightaway.   ☐

e) That's fine, as long as we all have enough workspace.   ☐

f) How often would that be?   ☐

g) Well, in fact they're included in my CV.   ☐

Past abilities

C Study the examples. Then complete the dialogues below with *could* or *was able to*.

- *could* (general ability)

  A: Can you use a PC?

  B: Yes, I can. In fact, I *could* use a PC when I was 10!

- *was able to* (one occasion)

  A: So were you late for the interview?

  B: No. Sue gave me a lift, so I *was able to* get there in time.

1 A: What foreign languages can you speak?

   B: I .... speak Italian quite fluently when I was a child but I've forgotten a lot.

2 A: What was your greatest achievement in your previous job?

   B: Well, I .... reorganise the Sales Department in a month.

3 A: What did you like best about your previous job?

   B: My boss really trusted me so I .... use my own initiative.

4 A: So you worked in Turkey three years ago. Could you give us some details?

   B: Certainly. As a matter of fact, I .... win a very big contract.

5 A: So how did the interview go?

   B: Fine, I think. I .... answer all the questions!

WRITING

Curriculum vitae

A **Complete Antonia's CV with the headings from the box.**

Achievements   ~~Address~~   E-mail   Experience   Interests   Personal details
Profile   Qualifications   Referees   Special skills   Telephone

Curriculum Vitae
Antonia Sophia Mehditash

........Address........[1] Rua Humberto Madeira 23, P – 3004-520, Coimbra, Portugal

........................[2] +351 239 856 207

........................[3] a.s.mehditash@netvisao.pt

........................[4]

An Assistant Marketing Director in a medium-sized company, Orey Tours, seeking a more challenging position with more responsibility. Able to work on own initiative to tight deadlines.

........................[5]

- Contributed to the development of a successful sales strategy
- Coordinated the work of the sales, marketing and advertising personnel
- Designed Excel spreadsheets for sales records

........................[6]

- Negotiating contracts with foreign and domestic airlines
- Working as part of a team
- Proficient user of MS Windows, MS Excel, Adobe InDesign, Dreamweaver, JavaScript

........................[7]

2005 – date	Assistant Marketing Director (Orey Tours, Coimbra)
July – Sept 2004	Work placement at Portugália Airlines (London office)

........................[8]

2002–2004	MBA at Brentford College (UK / Distance course)
1998–2002	BA in Economics at the University of Coimbra

........................[9]

Date of birth:	6th June 1979
Driving licence:	Full, clean

........................[10]

I sing in a choir and play basketball in an amateur team.

........................[11]

Ana Luisa Santos	Ms Celia Gutlerner
Professor of Economics	Director MBA Programmes
Avenida do Brasil 27	Brentford College
P – 1600 Lisboa	27 Burrard Street
Tel: +351 1 722 0893	Brentford TW9 0AK
Email: alsantos@netcabo.pt	Email: Gutlerner@BCMBA.ac.uk

B **Which heading in the CV in exercise A would you put each of these items under?**

1 2001: IELTS Certificate (Academic) – Overall Band 8   ....*Qualifications*.........

2 Designed Orey's website   ....

3 Excellent conversational Spanish and some French   ....

4 I also enjoy helping other people design their websites.   ....

5 Also an excellent team worker.   ....

Applying for a job

C **This draft letter of application is not appropriate. Rewrite it using some of the expressions from the Useful language box. Make any other necessary changes.**

> Hello
> I saw your ad in our local paper last week, so I want to apply for the job of Communications Assistant. I know I am the person you're looking for. I just got various A levels from school and all my friends say they love chatting with me. So write soon and tell me if you want to know more about me.
>
> Regards

USEFUL LANGUAGE	
Dear Sir or Madam,	Please let me know if there are any other details
With reference to your advertisement in ...	you need.
I would like to apply for the position of ...	I enclose a copy of my CV.
I feel I am well qualified for the position because ...	A full CV is attached.
I would be happy to give you more details and can be	I look forward to hearing from you.
contacted at any time.	Yours faithfully,

Editing

D **Read the text about how to prepare for a job interview.**

In each line **1–6** there is **one wrong word**.

For each line, **underline the wrong word** in the text and **write the correct word** in the space provided.

Before you go for a job interview, make sure that you do your

homework. Find out as much as you <u>could</u> about the company,   1 ......*can*.......

about its history, about what it does, how many people it employ,   2 ....

and so on. During the interview, try to keeping to the point. Give   3 ....

complete answers but do not talk for longer then necessary.   4 ....

Finally, remember that you can ask the interviewer question. This   5 ....

will show that you are really interested for the opportunity.   6 ....

Companies

VOCABULARY | **A** | Use the prepositions *at*, *by*, *for*, *in*, *of*, *to* and *on* to complete the extract from a company report.

PINELCOM

Financial performance

Pinelcom is committed ....*to*.........[1] creating and delivering value – value to its customers, value to its employees and value to the region. Our success in moving towards this goal is most evident in the financial results for this year. Turnover ....[2] the close of the year was €83.5 million, that is an increase ....[3] 12 per cent over the previous year, and profits rose ....[4] 6 per cent ....[5] €7.3 million. In spite of fierce competition, we have increased our market share to almost 25 per cent. As a result, our share price has risen and is now ....[6] an all-time high ....[7] €11.6.

A huge increase ....[8] production and rising demand have had a positive effect ....[9] our cash flow. We are planning to start full production ....[10] our recently opened Polish subsidiary ....[11] May.

Finally, I would like to congratulate our staff on their outstanding performance. Thank you all once again ....[12] your continuing support of the company.

B | Match the companies to the industry sector they belong to.

1	Lenovo, Apple, Dell, Microsoft	a)	Electrical / Electronics
2	Bayer, Johnson & Johnson, Novartis	b)	Engineering
3	BMW, General Motors, Nissan, Toyota	c)	Banking and finance
4	HSBC, ING	d)	Pharmaceuticals / Chemicals
5	LG, Nokia, Samsung, Siemens	e)	IT (Information Technology)
6	AP Møller-Maersk, Qatar Airways, Ryanair	f)	Retail
7	Ikea, Tesco, Wal-Mart, Zara	g)	Transport

C | Read the sentences and write the missing letters to complete the words.

1 Human r e s o u r c e s deals with employees, keeps their records and helps with any problems they might have.

2 If someone is _ _ _ f-e _ _ _ oy _ _, it means that they don't work for only one company.

3 Cisco Systems is a famous American IT company which _ _ pp _ _ _ _ Internet equipment.

4 A company which owns another company is called a _ _ r _ _ _ company.

5 A _ _ bs _ _ _ _ _ _ is a company which is more than 50 per cent owned by another company.

6 The main building or location of a company or organisation is its _ _ _ d o _ _ _ _ e.

7 Banking and tourism belong to the _ _ _ v _ _ _ industry.

8 All the people who work in a particular country, industry, or factory are called the _ _ _ kf _ _ _ _.

LANGUAGE REVIEW

Present tenses

A Match each sentence with the meaning expressed by the verb in *italics*.

1 American Express *provides* travel and financial services.
2 Ms Delgado *is replacing* Sandra as Office Manager until next Friday.
3 We *are improving* our services to meet the needs of a much wider range of customers.
4 We *are opening* our sixth subsidiary next month.
5 We *need* a different set of skills to address our company's challenges.
6 We *observe* our customers' reactions carefully.

a) temporary situation
b) future arrangement
c) ongoing situation
d) routine activity
e) factual information
f) verb usually used only in the present simple

B Correct the three sentences that use the wrong present tense.

1 What do you do on Friday morning?
2 We rarely raise our prices by more than 3 per cent.
3 Karlo is staying in Shanghai until the end of the conference.
4 Our largest subsidiary, based in Berlin, is going through a difficult period.
5 Our company looks for a new sales manager.
6 At the moment, we are not knowing the profit figures.

C Complete the text with the correct form (present simple or present continuous) of verbs from the box.

| attend | ~~coordinate~~ | go | have | know | prepare | speak | think | travel |

Leandra Korakis is Marketing Manager at Kayavis Food & Wine S.A., an expanding medium-sized business in Thessaloniki. She ...*coordinates*....[1] the work of a team of seven people. Kayavis ....[2] distributors in eleven countries in Europe and America so Leandra often ....[3] abroad. Next week, she ....[4] to Canada to visit their new retail outlet. She ....[5] Greek, English and Danish. At the moment she ....[6] an intensive German course because the owner of Kayavis ....[7] of opening a shop and a large restaurant in Frankfurt. Leandra ....[8] that she will have to work in Germany for six months so she ....[9] herself for her new assignment as best she can.

D Make questions for these answers. All the information is in the text in exercise C.

1 ......*What does Leandra do?*...... She coordinates the work of a team of seven people.
2 .... Eleven.
3 .... Next week.
4 .... To visit their new retail outlet.
5 .... Greek, English and Danish.
6 .... Because she will have to work in Germany.
7 .... In Frankfurt.

WRITING

Informal e-mails

A **Read the tip. Then number the sentences of the informal e-mail in the correct order.**

Tips

Remember that in business correspondence, information is often presented in the following order:

- appropriate greeting
- thanks and / or reference to previous contact
- main point
- other point(s)
- reference to future contact
- appropriate ending

From:	supersound@ntlworld.com
To:	Rik_Barneveld@ntlworld.nl; sandraverdonck@planet.nl
Subject:	Our next meeting

a) I'm attaching the draft agenda here for your information. ☐

b) Best wishes, ☐

c) If there are any points you'd like to add, please let me know. ☐

d) Many thanks for your latest mail and your useful ideas about our investment options. ☐

e) Dear Rik & Sandra, 1

f) Looking forward to seeing you both on 14th June. ☐

g) Our investment plan will certainly be the main focus of our next meeting, which is scheduled for 14th June. ☐

h) Ya Ling 8

B **Write Rik's reply (50–70 words) to Ya Ling's e-mail in exercise A.**

- Include the points in the tip.
- In addition, suggest that setting up online sales should be on the agenda and say why.

From:	Rik_Barneveld@ntlworld.nl
To:	supersound@ntlworld.com
Subject:	14th June meeting

Hi Ya Ling,

....

....

....

Editing **C** **Read Sandra's reply to Ya Ling's e-mail.**

In five of the lines **1–10** there is **one wrong word**. Five lines, however, are correct.

If a line is **correct**, put a tick (✓) in the space provided.

If there is a **wrong word** in the line, **underline the wrong word** in the text and **write the correct word** in the space provided.

From:	sandraverdonck@planet.nl
To:	supersound@ntlworld.com
Subject:	14th June meeting

Hello Ya Ling,

<u>Thanks</u> you for informing me about the meeting and for the agenda attached.	1	Thank
I am very sorry to tell you that, unfortunately, I won't be able to make 14th June	2	✓
because of previous engagements. We have been looking for a new Office	3	....
Manager for our Utrecht subsidiary for almost a month and we have now	4	....
shortlisted seven candidates. I'll be away 12th–15th June to interview they, as	5	....
well as to sort out a couple of other matters related to the lease of our offices.	6	....
As I can't be there in person, I'm attach some ideas for the investment plan. I	7	....
hope they are of some use. I have also made some suggestion for the agenda.	8	....
Good luck with the meeting. I hope it goes as well as the April one!	9	....
Once again, please accept my apologise for not being there with you all.	10	....

Best wishes,

Sandra

Linking ideas **D** **Complete the sentences with *because*, *but* or *so*.**

1 The motivation of the sales staff is now increasing ..... because ..... we bought some
   new company cars.

2 It is a difficult time for the industry .... our company is still growing.

3 Sales are falling .... management does not seem very worried about it.

4 Sales were not as good as they had hoped .... they launched
   a marketing campaign.

5 The best option is to buy new machinery .... the old machines
   are always breaking down.

6 There is a steady growth in sales .... profits are not rising.

7 Local competition is extremely strong .... we are planning to buy out
   two local competitors.

8 We are planning to open a new store in New York next year ....
   we want a foothold in the US market.

9 We increased our market share considerably .... our share price rose to
   an all-time high.

10 We were unable to finance the new project .... of severe cash
    flow problems.

Selling

VOCABULARY   **Use the clues to complete the crossword puzzle.**

Across

1   A .... is something you buy cheaply or for less than the usual price. (7)

6   A money-back .... is a promise to return the money paid for a product or service if the customer is not satisfied. (9)

7   If the goods you require are out of ...., they are not available. (5)

8   If you buy goods in ...., you buy large amounts of them. (4)

9   Always .... the small print before you sign a sales contract. (4)

12 Your credit card .... are the name, number and expiry date on your credit card. (7)

13 A .... is a person or company that sells goods in large quantities to businesses. (10)

Down

2   A .... is a company or a person that sells goods to members of the public. (8)

3   .... is a formal word meaning *buy*. (8)

4   To .... means to give someone their money back (e.g. because they are not satisfied with what they have bought). (6)

5   To .... means to send goods to a place. (8)

10 An .... is a request by a customer for goods or services. (5)

11 A .... is a large area where there are lots of shops, usually a covered area where cars cannot go. (4)

LANGUAGE REVIEW

Modals

A **Match each sentence to the meaning expressed by the modal in *italics*.**

1 You *should* order online, it's more convenient.
2 We *have to* work very hard to reach our sales targets.
3 You *mustn't* show your PIN to anyone.
4 The supermarket is just down the road so we *don't have to* take the car.

a) It is not necessary.
b) It would be a good idea.
c) It is necessary.
d) Don't do that!

B **Rewrite these sentences using an appropriate modal to replace the words in *italics*.**

1 If you want to be an effective salesperson, *it is necessary to* know how to deal with people.
   If you want to be an effective salesperson, ...*you have to*............ know how to deal with people.

2 *It is a good idea* for retailers to dispatch orders quickly.
   Retailers ....

3 One of the good things about malls is that *it is not necessary to* walk a lot from one shop to another.
   One of the good things about malls is that .... walk a lot from one shop to another.

4 *It is not a good idea to* talk a lot about yourself.
   You ....

5 If you order before 15th April, *it's not necessary* for you to pay until August.
   If you order before 15th April, you ....

6 This deal is very important for all of us, *so no mistakes please*!
   This deal is very important so we .... !

7 It is against the law to sell these medicines to anyone who hasn't got a prescription.
   You .... a prescription if you want to buy these medicines.

C **Match the sentence halves.**

1 We were all in agreement
2 Her new flat is near her workplace
3 We didn't have any more paper in stock
4 They usually order online
5 They don't have an online catalogue
6 They say some of the goods are damaged

a) which means they don't have to queue!
b) so we'll have to exchange them.
c) so we didn't have to discuss the deal any further.
d) so she won't have to drive to work anymore.
e) so we had to order some more.
f) so we have to ask them to send us one.

D **Complete the table with the verbs from the sentence halves a–f in exercise C.**

Past	Present	Future
....	*don't have to*	....
....	....	....

WRITING

Placing an order

A Complete the online order form with items from the box.

5	10	50	83.23	155	1,581.27
Edinburgh	T-shirts	Tim Atkinson	~~Unit price~~		

BEBOP TENNISGEAR * SECURE ONLINE ORDER FORM**

Quantity	Item	Code	*Unit price* [1]	Total cost
1	Ball machine	BM/709	€ 750	€ 750
................[2]	'Champion' rackets	RCH43	€ 55	€ 550
50	'Tournament' balls	TB	€ 3.10	€ ....[3]
................[4]	'Regular' balls	RB	€ 2.49	€ 124.50
................[5]	Gear bags	B27-H	€ 10	€ 50
10	................[6]	T/12	€ 3.50	€ 35
			Gross total	€ 1,664.50
			Discount @ 5%	€ ....[7]
			Net amount due	€ ....[8]

Name: ....[9]

Company: Atkinson's Ultimate Sports Centre

Address: 45 Dalston Gardens

................[10]

Post code: EH5 5EY

Phone: 0131 548 8937

E-mail: atkinson@btinternet.com

THANK YOU!

Replying to an order

B These phrases are often used when replying to an order. Complete them with words from the box.

deliver	doing	hesitate	~~placing~~	receipt

- Thank you for ..... *placing* .....[1] an order with (name of the company).
- Thank you for your order of (date).
- We confirm ....[2] of your order dated (date).
- Shipping normally takes two to three days / a week / etc.
- We can ....[3] within a week / a month / etc.
- Do not ....[4] to contact us if you need further information / details.
- If you have any queries, please contact us.
- We look forward to receiving further orders from you.
- Looking forward to ....[5] business with you again.

C Choose one from each pair of items in the box to complete this formal e-mail.

> We look forward to doing / We hope we can do   All the best / Yours sincerely
>
> things / goods   Dear / Hello   Thanks / Thank you   Just to say / We confirm

---

To: atkinson@btinternet.com
Cc: bebopaccounts@easynet.co.uk
Subject: Your order 21/GT06

.....................¹ Mr Atkinson,

.....................² for your order of 21st June.

.....................³ that you have ordered the following items from our online catalogue:

1	Ball machine	BM/709
10	'Champion' rackets	RCH43
50	'Tournament' balls	TB
50	'Regular' balls	RB
5	Gear bags	B27-H
10	T-shirts	T/12

We are now dealing with your order.
The sum of €1,581.27 has been charged to your credit card and the ....⁴
will be shipped on 24th June.

If you have any queries, please contact us at bebopsales@easynet.co.uk.

.....................⁵ business with you again.

.....................⁶,

Neelum Singh

Editing

D Read the text about writing business e-mails.

In most of the lines **1–9** there is **one extra word** which does not fit. Some lines, however, are correct.

If a line is **correct**, put a tick (✓) in the space provided.

If there is an **extra word** in the line, write that word in the space provided.

Basically, the rules for writing business e-mails and letters are the same:	1 ....✓.........
be clear, be so polite and do not write more than you have to. Over the	2 ....so.........
past ten years, business correspondence has generally become a simpler	3 ....
and more informal, and this tendency is even more visible in e-mails. But	4 ....
some things they have not changed. Clarity of layout is still important so	5 ....
you should to use paragraphs and space them out. Grammar and spelling	6 ....
too need to be accurate and if you want to make a good impression on	7 ....
your business partners. Even the best spellchecker cannot find all the	8 ....
mistakes you make so always to check your e-mails carefully.	9 ....

Great ideas

VOCABULARY **A** Match a verb from box A with a noun from box B to complete the sentences below. Use a suitable form of the verb–noun combination.

A	B
to develop	the environment
to extend	advantage of (something)
to make	a (product) range
to meet	a business idea
to protect	a breakthrough
to take	a need
to win	an award

1 Brainstorming is an effective way of ..... *developing a business idea* ....

2 A couple of years ago, scientists .... in the treatment of cancer.

3 'Eco-consumers' choose companies which do not produce a lot of toxic waste and have a clear policy of ....

4 Sometimes an idea may simply be when a company .... an opportunity to offer more choice to its customers.

5 If one of your products .... for innovation, prospective customers may see you as a dynamic, high-quality company and decide to choose you over your competitors.

6 Our company would like to attract a wider variety of customers, that's why we are planning to .... of cosmetics and toiletries.

7 A good business idea is one that generates profits and at the same time ....

B Complete each set of sentences with the same word.

1 The marketing department wants to ..... *hold* ...... a meeting next week.
   We are planning to ..... *hold* ...... our next sales conference in Mumbai.
   Do you know which animals ..... *hold* ...... the record for the longest migration?

2 During lectures, it's a good idea if you .... notes as you listen.
   The main goal of any business is to .... money.
   She wants to .... some suggestions about improving our database.

3 Industrialised countries should try to .... waste instead of exporting it.
   The best way to .... competition is to buy out your main competitors.
   Pollution is a big problem in our city and we are trying all sorts of ideas to .... it.

4 We plan to offer free ice cream to all consumers one day a year to .... awareness of the company.
   Our cars come in two colours. If you want extra colours, I'm afraid we have to .... the price by 5 per cent.
   Some people buy luxury products because such products .... their status and give them a new, more upmarket image.

5 I can't find a solution to all problems, of course, but I..................... my best.
  A lot of people want to..................... part-time work when they retire.
  We..................... a lot of business with Chinese telecommunications companies.

6 If you continue to be late for work, you will..................... the sack.
  All members of staff..................... an end-of-year bonus.
  I'll talk to the manager during the break if I..................... the chance.

LANGUAGE REVIEW

Past tenses

A Match the sentence halves.

1 They were still working on their new designs

2 As they had an exciting idea to promote,

3 They invited high-profile entrepreneurs on TV

4 Apple released the first iPad in April 2010

5 We were having a boring meeting

6 An Australian entrepreneur expressed interest in the new product

a) that they were exhibiting at the Inventors' Fair.

b) when suddenly Jackson announced that he was stepping down as General Manager.

c) when they saw an opening in the market.

d) they decided to exhibit at the Inventors' Fair.

e) and asked them to talk about innovation and change.

f) and sold 3 million of the devices in 80 days.

B Correct the sentences that use the wrong past tense.

1 Because Hiltex was worried that its competitors would copy its new machines, it was immediately filing patents for them.
   Because Hiltex was worried that its competitors would copy its new machines, it immediately filed patents for them.

2 At first, the agency was not believing that the machine would save so much time.

3 I was planning to visit the International Inventors' Fair but I did not have time.

4 The story goes that Professor Auenberg was having the idea for the electric shoebrush while he was washing up.

5 They failed to see the gap in the market and so missed a unique opportunity.

6 Z40, the new drug developed by Pharmatek, marked a breakthrough in the treatment of cancer.

7 Zirkon already made good profits when it introduced its new digital camera in 2010.

8 Last year, we spent a lot on marketing and so attracted a lot of new customers.

C Complete the sentences with the correct form (past simple or past continuous) of the verbs in brackets.

1 Our company ...*was losing*... (lose) money at an alarming rate but then in 2010 we..................... (launch) our Hermes 5 tablet computer. Sales..................... (go up) dramatically and our financial situation..................... (improve) rapidly.

2 We..................... (have) a successful negotiation when suddenly our boss..................... (phone) us to say he..................... (want) completely different conditions.

3 We..................... (plan) to patent our new drug but we..................... (wait) far too long. A month after our discovery, our main competitor..................... (sell) basically the same product.

4 Julia .... (*decide*) to take a few months off in 2001, when she
.... (*work*) for Clairval Cosmetics. While she .... (*tour*)
New Zealand, she .... (*develop*) an interest in Maori culture. She
.... (*take*) samples of some of the plants used in their rituals because
she .... (*believe*) they could be used in some of her company's products.

WRITING

Giving information

A **Put the lines of the message in the correct order.**

a)	I want to take our 15 Spanish visitors	1
b)	as they are leaving early on Monday morning.	
c)	of the Spanish version of the catalogue.	
d)	opening hours, entrance fee and price	
e)	Please find out the following for me:	
f)	to the Exhibition of Inventions on Sunday	

B **Write a reply to the message in exercise A, based on the following information.**

International Exhibition of Inventions, New Techniques and Products

Geneva, Palexpo 1st–5th May

USEFUL INFORMATION
Dates: 1st–5th May

Place: Palexpo, Geneva

Opening hours:
Wednesday–Saturday: 10 a.m. to 7 p.m.
Sunday: 10 a.m. to 6 p.m.

Admission charges:
Adults: Fr12.00
Children under the age of 15: Fr8.00
Groups of 10 or more persons: Fr8.00 per person
Tickets available at the doors of the exhibition.

Official catalogue:
Contains a description of all the inventions (available
in French, German and English): Fr25.00

Hotel reservation:
Central Tourist Office
P.O. Box 1649 - CH - 1244 Genève 1
Tel: 004122 908 73 24
Fax: 004122 908 73 25

Please contact your nearest travel agent for special rates.
Quote the name of the event and the code IDS 39K.

Message:

On Sunday, the International Exhibition is open from ....

....

....

C You work for a large insurance company which always has a lot of confidential documents to destroy. At the Exhibition of Inventions you saw a new type of shredder. Write an e-mail (75–85 words) to your Head of Department, including:

- details about the machine
  - shreds paper and cardboard
  - fully automatic
  - fitted with energy-saving device
  - very quiet
- why you think it would be a good idea to buy this machine
- where your Head of Department might get further information.

To: Montse Balaguer
Re: Document shredder
Date: 7th May

Dear Montse,

....

....

Editing

D Read this text about Jeff Bezos, the founder of Amazon.

In seven of the lines **1–10** there is **one extra word** which does not fit. Three lines, however, are correct.

If a line is **correct**, put a tick (✓) in the space provided.

If there is an **extra word** in the line, write that word in the space provided.

Jeff Bezos was just 31 when he launched Amazon.com in 1995. The road to	1 ....✓.......
success was long and hard but his company later it became the internet's biggest	2 ....it.......
retailer, with the revenues of almost $2bn and a customer base of over 10 million.	3 ....
To his fans, Bezos is a visionary, a retail revolutionary in the tradition of Richard	4 ....
Sears, whose mail-order business was changed American shopping in the late	5 ....
19th and early 20th centuries. 'He saw the future in a concrete way before they	6 ....
anyone else did', says Brad Silverberg, co-founder of a Seattle-based and venture	7 ....
capital firm. 'He has done more than anyone else never in the world to change	8 ....
people's buying habits. People go to the web and buy stuff because of Jeff	9 ....
Bezos. He created a household word – that's for an amazing accomplishment.' To	10 ....
many, Bezos will always remain the man who taught the world to shop online.	

Stress

VOCABULARY **A** Choose the best word (a, b or c) to complete each space.

The dictionary defines stress as 'a continuous feeling of worry that prevents you from relaxing.' At work there are a lot of potentially stressful situations. For example, having to ....*lead*........[1] a formal meeting or ....[2] a presentation to senior executives can cause stress, especially the first time. In fact, all kinds of situations are more stressful when you have never found yourself in them before. However, experience does not always solve the problem. Indeed, many people say that they always feel under stress when ....[3] a valuable contract or meeting important visitors from abroad or even just when working to ....[4] deadlines. Other situations that employees generally find difficult to cope with include dealing with a customer who has a ....[5] and asking the boss for a pay ....[6].

All the situations mentioned above are examples of short-term stress. Experts agree that this kind of stress is less damaging to health than long-term stress, which happens when employees constantly work ....[7] pressure or have to cope with an ever-increasing ....[8]. In such cases, a complete change of ....[9] can, of course, be a solution but companies should try to reduce stress levels before their employees are severely ....[10] otherwise absenteeism may increase and some staff may even decide to ....[11].

1 a) direct	b) go	c) lead (circled)
2 a) make	b) speak	c) show
3 a) dealing	b) negotiating	c) transferring
4 a) sharp	b) tight	c) narrow
5 a) complaint	b) complaining	c) complain
6 a) rising	b) bargain	c) rise
7 a) on	b) in	c) under
8 a) workload	b) workforce	c) workaholic
9 a) life cycle	b) lifestyle	c) work–life balance
10 a) worked out	b) overworked	c) worked over
11 a) recruit	b) resign	c) participate

B Complete the sentences with the correct prepositions.

1 Being stuck ....*in*.......... a traffic jam on your way .... work can be quite stressful, especially if you have an important appointment.

2 In Ireland, ... example, the economy is shrinking and business owners are worried .... how they will keep their business alive.

3 Gentaro is part .... a multinational company based .... Milan.

4 I wish I could relax a bit more instead .... having to work .... strict deadlines all the time.

5 Lisa worked until 11 o'clock .... night to meet the deadline .... presenting the report.

6 Mike says going .... a stress counsellor is out .... the question.

LANGUAGE REVIEW

The present perfect tense

A Three business people were asked about stressful experiences. Look at the table then answer the questions using short answers.

Have you ever ...	... asked your boss for a pay rise?	... led a formal meeting?	... negotiated a very valuable contract?
Sergio	✗	✓	✗
Marie	✓	✗	✓
Lucy	✓	✗	✗

1 Has Sergio ever led a formal meeting? *Yes he has.*

2 Has Sergio ever asked his boss for a pay rise? *No, he hasn't.*

3 Has Marie ever negotiated a very valuable contract? ....

4 Has Marie ever led a formal meeting? ....

5 Have Lucy and Sergio ever negotiated a very valuable contract? ....

6 Have Lucy and Marie ever asked their boss for a pay rise? ....

7 Has anybody ever led a formal meeting? ....

B Now read about other people's stressful experiences and make questions for the answers.

Have you ever ...	... been late for an important event?	... taken part in a conference call?	... dealt with an aggressive customer?
Heinrich ♂	✓	✗	✗
Yaling ♀	✗	✗	✓
Ahmed ♂	✓	✗	✓

1 *Has Yaling ever been late for an important event?*

No, she hasn't.

2 *Have Heinrich and Ahmed ever been late for an important event?*

Yes, they have.

3 *Has Yaling ever dealt with*

Yes, she has.

4 *Has Heinrich ever dealt with*

No, he hasn't.

5 *Have H&A ever taken part*

No, they haven't.

6 *Has Y ever taken part*

No, she hasn't.

C Complete the text with the correct form (past simple or present perfect) of the verbs in brackets.

I *'ve worked* [1] (work) for Dat@ready since last summer. So far it *has been* [2] (be) enjoyable and I *haven't had* [3] (not /have) any difficulties. At the beginning I *expected* [4] (expect) to have a lot of problems, though. I *thought* [5] (think) I might not get on with my colleagues but all of them *have been* [6] (be) friendly and supportive since the very first day. Last week, for example, I *had to* [7] (have to) meet some tight deadlines, which *was* [8] (be) quite stressful. One of my colleagues *offered* [9] (offer) to collect all the data I *needed* [10] (need) for the quarterly report. This *saved* [11] (save) me at least half a day's work. I *'ve worked* [12] (work) in four different companies over the last ten years but I *have never felt* [13] (never /feel) so welcome as at Dat@ready, I must say.

WRITING

Punctuation

A **Rewrite the article, using punctuation and capital letters where necessary.**

> according to a recent survey over 14 per cent of all employed people in the eu suffer from stress two of the main reasons are overwork and fear of redundancy in addition a large number of employees are suffering from headaches backache and chest pains because of overcrowded offices poor ventilation and badly designed furniture and equipment over the last few years this has resulted in increased levels of absenteeism and a gradual decrease in productivity

B **Put each set of words in the correct order to make a sentence.**

1 a) at some point / in their life. / stress / Everyone experiences
Everyone experiences stress at some point in their life.

  b) handle stress / But men and / very differently. / women generally
But men and women generally handle stress very differently.

2 a) men than / from stress-related illnesses. / women suffer / However, more
....

  b) as good / coping strategies / as women's. / That is / are not / because their
....

3 a) come from / from work. / home and / These pressures
....

  b) are only / at work. / many men / under pressure / By contrast,
....

4 a) are much / than men. / To begin / more flexible / with, women
....

  b) with the / Also, they / than men. / pressures better / usually cope
....

C **Put the four pairs of sentences in exercise B in the best order to make a paragraph.**

1 ☐ ☐ ☐

Reports

D **Look at the graph and complete the sentences a–f with the correct form (present simple, past simple or present perfect) of the verbs in brackets. Then number the sentences in the correct order to make a report for the International Health Symposium.**

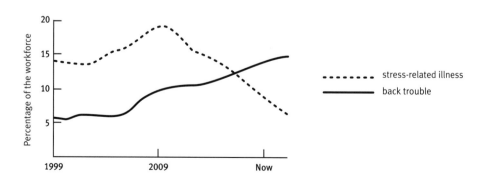

1   **a)** The graph .....*shows*....... (*show*) the changes in the percentage of the workforce staying off work because of back trouble and stress-related illness.   ☐ 1

4   **b)** Secondly, absences caused by stress-related illness .*showed*......... (*show*) a similar trend in the period 1999–2009. They ...*increased*... (*increase*) by 3 per cent, to reach 17 per cent in 2009.   ☐ 4

6   **c)** In conclusion, back trouble is still a problem today but we ..*have made*.. (*make*) excellent progress in bringing down the percentage of the workforce absent from work because of stress.   ☐ 6

2   **d)** To begin with, we can see that absences caused by back trouble *have risen*.. (*rise*) gradually since 1999.   ☐ 2

5   **e)** Since 2009, however, they .*have fallen*.. (*fall*) dramatically and now ......*stand*..... (*stand*) at 6 per cent.   ☐ 5

3   **f)** Their percentage ..*went up*.. (*go up*) from 6 per cent in 1999 to 11 per cent ten years later and it now ....*stands*.... (*stand*) at about 13 per cent.   ☐ 3

USEFUL LANGUAGE	
The graph / table / slide shows … As you can see from this graph / table / slide … Firstly, … To begin with, …	To conclude, … In conclusion, … Secondly, … Next, … Finally, …

E   **Your boss, Slawa Kowalska, wanted you to take part in an important seminar tomorrow morning. You cannot go because you have a terrible headache. In fact, you have not slept very well for a week. Write a message (60–80 words) to your boss.**

- Apologise and say why you cannot attend.
- Tell her what you plan to do about your health.

> **Message**:
> To: Slawa Kowalska
> From: ....
> ....

Editing   **F**   **Read the text about stress at work.**

In each line **1–6** there is **one wrong word**.

For each line, **underline the wrong word** in the text and **write the correct word** in the space provided.

Reducing stress is in the interest of both employers and employees.

First of all, less stress <u>mean</u> more productivity because, as everybody knows, the   1 ....*means*......

results of stress are often illness and absent from work. Every year, millions   2 ....

of days of work is lost because of stress and stress-related illness.   3 ....

As regards employees, on the other hand, a lower level of stress leading not only to   4 ....

increased job satisfaction but also to best relationships at work and at home.   5 ....

Of course, it also contributes a great deal to a generally feeling of happiness.   6 ....

UNIT **6** Entertaining

A Complete the story with the words from the box.

aperitif	bill	book	cash	cosy	course	delicious	dessert	dishes
efficient	~~entertain~~	guest	marketing	menu	negotiate	order		
recommended	relax	starter	variety					

As I had to ...*entertain*..[1] an important visitor from abroad, I asked different colleagues if they knew a good restaurant in town. They all ....[2] 'Mirella's Garden'. 'Very ....[3] atmosphere,' they said, 'the food is absolutely ....[4] and the service is very ....[5].'

It was quite busy when we arrived. Fortunately, I had asked my assistant to ....[6] a table in advance. From where we were seated, we had a stunning view across the lake. My ....[7], Mr Yared, seemed quite pleased, so I began to ....[8]. I suggested having an ....[9] but he said he hardly ever drank alcohol, and certainly never on working days. I hoped I hadn't made a gaffe! We looked at the lunch ....[10], which had a wide ....[11] of typical ....[12] from our region.

When the waiter came to take our ....[13], Mr Yared surprised me once more. He had chosen stuffed mushrooms as a ....[14] but he wanted to have them served *after* the main ....[15]. 'This is not a funny custom from my country,' he said with a smile, 'just a personal preference.'

The food was indeed superb. Mr Yared spoke about his family and his hobbies and asked about mine. We talked only briefly about the contract we had to ....[16] that afternoon.

As it was getting late, we didn't have a ....[17], just coffee, and then I asked for the ....[18]. But when I reached for my wallet, I realised to my horror that I didn't have it on me. Of course – it was at home, in my other jacket. No ....[19] or credit card – how embarrassing! The only solution I could think of was to ask the manager to call MCI, my company. 'MCI? Is that Micro Computers International?' the manager asked. Indeed it was. 'No need to phone, sir; we'll put this on your account,' the manager continued. 'MCI has had an account with us for three years. My wife is MCI's ....[20] Director.' Mr Yared and I looked at each other and we both burst out laughing. The day was saved.

B Choose the best word (a, b or c) to complete each sentence.

1 Many people have only two .....*meals*..... a day: breakfast and dinner.
   a) meals   b) dishes   c) courses

2 Jane invited me round for dinner last night. Her husband is a wonderful ....
   a) cooker   b) dish   c) cook

3 Tom worked in Bangkok for a year and now he is very keen on Thai ....
   a) kitchen   b) dish   c) cuisine

4 They are vegetarians so we should not buy any ....
   a) meal   b) meat   c) food

5 This chocolate mousse is delicious. Could I have the ....?
   a) recipe   b) cookbook   c) receipt

C **Cross out the odd-one-out in each set. Explain your choice.**

1 cabbage / ~~venison~~ / cucumber / broccoli / spinach
All the other words are names of vegetables.

2 roast / baked / boiled / grilled / fried / bottled

3 medium-rare / well-done / excellent / rare

4 draught / healthy / spicy / salty / rich / fattening

LANGUAGE REVIEW

Multiword verbs

A **Match the sentence halves.**

1 Last week, I had to look — a) come over and see them in Antalya.
2 First, I showed them around b) the Old Town.
3 I certainly look forward — c) after five clients from Turkey.
4 I hope I can take d) on really well.
5 One of them did not turn e) to a very good restaurant.
6 The food was delicious and we all got f) to seeing them all again.
7 Then, I took them out g) up their invitation next summer.
8 They said I should h) up, unfortunately.

B **Put the sentences from exercise A in the correct order to make a story.**

[1] [5] [ ] [ ] [ ] [ ] [ ] [ ]

C **Use the explanation in brackets to choose the correct multiword verb from the box. Then use the correct form of the verb to complete the sentences.**

| carry out   come up with   give up   hold on   ~~look for~~ |
| put off   put through   set up   turn down |

1 We ... *looked for* ... a new sales manager with at least three years' experience. (*tried to find*)

2 The government is encouraging people to .... new businesses. (*start*)

3 Rick thought March was too early for our seminar so he .... it .... until May. (*arranged to have it at a later date*)

4 Unfortunately, we had to .... their invitation because we had another engagement. (*refuse*)

5 Carol .... a well-paid job to train as a social worker. (*stopped doing*)

6 We are .... a survey to find out what kind of restaurants are most popular with businesspeople. (*doing*)

7 Can you .... ? I'm trying to .... you .... (*wait / connect*)

8 It was a very productive meeting. We all .... new ideas for our next advertising campaign. (*thought of*)

WRITING
Reports

A Two thousand executives from different countries named their three favourite forms of entertainment when they are abroad on business. Look at the bar chart showing the results of the survey then complete the report with the phrases from the box.

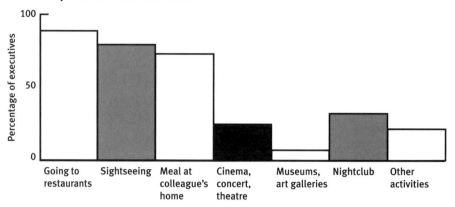

| almost as many | far less frequently | finally | secondly | ~~the bar chart shows~~ |
| the most popular activity | with a very small number |

.....*The bar chart shows*...[1] how popular certain forms of entertainment are with executives while they are abroad on business. ....[2] is clearly going to restaurants: 85 per cent of the executives interviewed mentioned it in their top three. ....[3], seeing the sights was mentioned by 75 per cent of the respondents and ....[4] said they enjoyed being invited round to a colleague's home for a meal.

Other forms of entertainment were mentioned ....[5]. About 25 per cent of the respondents enjoy going to a nightclub and 20 per cent to the cinema, the theatre or a concert. Museums and art galleries are popular ....[6] of executives: only about 5 per cent.

....[7], other activities, with included playing tennis, guided tours and wine or beer tasting, were mentioned by 15 per cent of the respondents.

Hotel bookings

B Your company is organising a one-day conference on Friday 6th June. You are expecting delegates from your overseas branches. Match the sentence halves in this e-mail from the Canadian branch.

To: BMarks@easynet.co.uk
From: Jim.Byrne@lycos.com

1 Could you book one single room   **a)** and leaving on the 7th in the morning.

2 If possible, he would prefer   **b)** but not too expensive?

3 He's arriving on Thursday 5th   **c)** a non-smoking room.

4 Don't book him into the Royal this time,   **d)** in the name of Robert Dorey.

5 Could you find him somewhere comfortable   **e)** it's too far from the centre.

Thanks.

Jim

C Look at the advertisement. Write a reply (30–40 words) to the e-mail in exercise B confirming the booking and giving some details about the hotel.

Astoria Hotel
☆ ☆ ☆

Double rooms from **£190**
Single rooms from **£110**
Prices include English or Continental Breakfast
Non-smoking 4th & 5th floors
Just a 5-minute walk from the city centre
The best value for money!

To: Jim.Byrne@lycos.com
From: BMarks@easynet.co.uk

Dear Jim,

....

....

....

Looking forward to Robert's visit.

Best wishes,

Brian

D Rewrite Robert's e-mail using paragraphs, punctuation and capital letters where necessary.

To: BMarks@easynet.co.uk
From: robdorey@lycos.com

---

dear brian this is to thank you for your hospitality during and after the conference you gave me a lot of your time and made my visit very memorable walking round the old town in the evening was really fascinating also i thought the food in that mediterranean restaurant where we had supper was just perfect it was a great pleasure to meet you if you come to canada i would like to return your kindness and generosity once again thank you regards robert

New business

VOCABULARY

A Complete each sentence with an appropriate economic term from the box.

> balance of trade   exchange rate   foreign investment
> government bureaucracy   gross domestic product (GDP)   inflation rate
> interest rate   labour force   tax incentives   unemployment rate

1 If you plan to borrow money, you will want to know the ...*interest rate*...

2 In countries where the ...*unempl. rate*... is high, young people tend to study more.

3 How many yen to the euro? Do you know the ...*exch. rate*..., by any chance?

4 According to a recent survey, 12 per cent of the ...*lab. force*... are earning less than the minimum wage.

5 So many forms to fill in just to import one photocopier! Nobody needs all this ...*gvt. bureaucracy*...

6 The higher the ...*GDP*... of a country, the richer its people are.

7 When the value of a country's exports is greater than the value of its imports, we say that the ...*bal. of trade*... is 'favourable'.

8 Prices increased again last month so the ...*inflation rate*... rose to 5.3 per cent.

9 Less government bureaucracy will encourage ...*foreign invest*...

10 The government is offering attractive ...*tax incentives*... to encourage foreign investment.

B Match the economic terms (1–6) to their definitions (a–f).

1 foreign debt
2 public expenditure
3 recession
4 subsidies
5 trade deficit
6 trade surplus

a) the total amount of money spent by a government on schools, roads, the army, etc.

b) money that a country owes to lenders abroad

c) situation when a country sells more goods to other countries than it buys from other countries

d) situation when a country pays more money for imports than it gets from exports

e) money that a government pays to make something cheaper to buy

f) a period when trade and business activity decreases

C Complete the sentences with economic terms from exercise B.

1 To help farmers, the EU has given out millions of euros in agricultural ...*subsidies*...

2 The country was able to repay some of its loans from abroad and so reduce its ...*foreign debt*...

3 Industrial production is still decreasing. It seems that the country is heading for a ...*recession*...

LANGUAGE REVIEW

Time clauses

A **Correct the sentences which are wrong. The first one has been done for you.**

1 We can't invest in that country until their economy will be stable.
We can't invest in that country until their economy is stable.

2 I'll let you know as soon as I receive their new brochure.

3 I'll let you know as soon as I've received their new brochure.

4 We'll phone you when the goods will be here.

5 When we've discussed the contract, we can close the meeting.

6 When we discuss the contract, we must remember to ask about transport costs.

7 We'll deal with insurance after they will tell us about their special discount.

8 Our guests would like to visit the production unit before they will go back to Qatar.

9 Before they sign this contract, they want us to promise better terms for future business.

10 I don't recommend investing there until they've reduced government bureaucracy.

B **Match the two parts of each dialogue.**

1 A: When do you want to discuss the project?

2 A: Have you read Peter's sales report?

3 A: So have they won the contract, then?

4 A: It seems we're not doing business with Alfatex anymore.

5 A: It would be useful to know today's exchange rates.

6 A: These figures need checking.

7 A: Are you going to the trade fair now?

a) B: No, never again. Certainly not until they apologise for their terrible mistakes.

b) B: We don't know yet. We'll have more information after we've talked to the team leader.

c) B: Yes, I agree. We'll find out as soon as we get the *FT*.

d) B: Yes, I have. I'd like to discuss it with you when you have a minute.

e) B: Yes. If anybody phones while I'm out, tell them I'll be back by 1.30.

f) B: Well, could we possibly do that before the meeting starts?

g) B: When you've typed them all up, we can check them together.

C **Make one sentence from the two sentences given.**

1 We'll meet all the candidates. Then we'll decide how many to employ.
After we've *met all the candidates, we'll decide how many to employ.*

2 Julia will finish her report soon. I want to see it immediately.
I .... as soon as ....

3 I will not invite them anymore. They must apologise first.
I .... until ....

4 Perhaps we'll employ him. Let's contact his referees first.
Let's .... before ....

5 I'll type up the report. Then I'll give you a copy.
I'll .... when I've ....

6 You'll be on the plane. Read the contracts then.
.... when ....

7 Prices are going to increase soon. Let's buy now.
.... before ....

8 We'll win the contract. We'll inform our shareholders immediately.
As soon as ...., ...

WRITING

Linking ideas

A Match each government measure with its purpose.

Government measure	Purpose
1 create free training programmes	a) attract foreign investors
2 make exports easier	b) stimulate consumer spending
3 pass a very strict environmental law	c) reduce the budget deficit
4 raise taxes	d) reduce unemployment
5 lower the interest rate	e) improve the balance of trade
6 reduce bureaucracy	f) stop companies polluting the air and water

B Express each of the ideas in exercise A in one sentence, using the linker *in order to*.

1 In order to reduce unemployment, the government is creating free training programmes. **or** The government is creating free training programmes in order to reduce unemployment.

2 The government is making ....

3 In order to stop companies ....

4 ....

5 ....

6 ....

Reports

C Look at the table and then correct the four numerical mistakes in the report about men employed. The first one has been done for you.

People employed in three industries by gender				
	Percentage			
	Men		Women	
Sector	2000	2010	2000	2010
Manufacturing	33	25	20	10
Health, education and public administration services	17	20	40	45
Financial and business services	10	15	10	20

REPORT

A third of all men employed were in manufacturing in 2000, compared with only a ~~fifth~~ in 2010.
quarter

On the other hand, around one in eight men employed were in health, education and public administration services in 2000, while the same industry accounted for one-fifth of men's jobs in 2010.

As regards the percentage of men employed in financial and business services, it increased from 12 per cent in 2000 to 15 per cent twenty years later.

D Use the table in exercise C to write a similar report (75–85 words) about *women* employed.

REPORT

One-fifth of all women employed ....

....

....

On the other hand, ...

....

....

As regards the percentage ....

....

....

Editing **E** Read this economic profile of a country.

In most of the lines **1–13** there is **one extra word** which does not fit. Some lines, however, are correct.

If a line is **correct**, put a tick (✓) in the space provided.

If there is an **extra word** in the line, write that word in the space.

Our country has become a completely modern market	1 ....✓........
economy. It is characterised by high-tech agriculture, the	2 ....the........
up-to-date industry and an extensive government welfare	3 ....
measures. Other features include very good living and	4 ....
standards, as well as high dependence on their foreign trade.	5 ....
We export food and the energy and have a comfortable	6 ....
balance of payments surplus. The government has reduced	7 ....
so the formerly high unemployment rate and maintained low	8 ....
inflation and a stable currency. It has also lowered income	9 ....
tax rates and raised environmental taxes. In this way so it has	10 ....
been able to maintain overall but tax revenues. Finally, in	11 ....
order to deal with long-term demographic changes which	12 ....
could reduce the labour force, the government it has	13 ....
introduced a number of labour market reforms.	

Marketing

VOCABULARY | **A** | **Use the clues to complete the crossword puzzle.**

Across

1 The percentage of sales a company or a product has is its market .... (5)

5 Companies sometimes promote their products by giving .... gifts to customers. (4)

6 Companies carry out market research to get information about what buyers .... and want. (4)

7 The life .... of a product is the length of time people continue to buy it. (5)

9 An advertising campaign takes place over a period of time and usually has a specific .... (3)

10 Good marketing should increase the volume of .... (5)

11 A company's sales target is how much it wants to .... in a certain period of time. (4)

Down

2 An advertising .... advises companies on advertising. (6)

3 A company's product .... is the set of products made by that particular company. (5)

4 A company's advertising .... is the amount of money available for advertising during a particular period. (6)

5 Sales .... show how much a company has sold over a certain period of time. (7)

8 Production .... are what a company must spend on production. (5)

9 Celebrities often appear in .... for clothes and cosmetics. (3)

B **Choose the best word (a, b or c) to complete each space in the text.**

The name game

A brand can be defined as a name given to a product by a company so that the product can easily be recognised by its name or its design. In our very _competitive_[1] business world, a good brand is one of the keys to the success of any company. It is often a powerful ....[2] tool.

However, the name is not everything. For a brand to be successful, marketers have to know what the consumer ....[3] and wants so a lot of market ....[4] is necessary. This gives them a 'consumer ....[5]', that is to say a kind of picture of the typical customer. It is a picture not only of the customer's needs and wants but also of their beliefs and values. If the brand then clearly reflects those values, it is more likely to be successful.

The customer has so much ....[6] nowadays that a good brand is a necessity so that one product is clearly different from another in his or her mind.

A good brand, of course, also has long-term benefits as it will ....[7] to many different market ....[8] and to people from different cultures.

1	a) informative		b) competitive (circled)	c)	conservative
2	a) sales		b) sell	c)	sold
3	a) wishes		b) needs	c)	orders
4	a) study		b) research	c)	science
5	a) summary		b) report	c)	profile
6	a) choice		b) option	c)	suggestion
7	a) attract		b) persuade	c)	appeal
8	a) shares		b) portions	c)	segments

A **Complete the questions with words from the box.**

| how long | how many | how much | what | ~~when~~ | which | who | why |

1 ..... _When_ ...... did you launch this advertising campaign?

2 .... didn't you contact an advertising agency?

3 .... money did you spend on the campaign?

4 .... new products did you launch? Was it two or three?

5 .... did you target your new product at?

6 .... market segments has your product been most successful in?

7 .... do you expect people to continue to buy this product?

8 .... is your sales forecast?

B **Match the Marketing Manager's responses (a–h) to the interviewer's questions in exercise A.**

a) Almost 20,000 euros. `3`

b) As I said, it's been doing extremely well and we expect a considerable increase in the winter. ☐

c) In late spring. ☐

d) So far it's been doing very well with middle-class males in their thirties to mid-fifties. ☐

e) We had health-conscious people in mind as well as the elderly. ☐

f) We think it will have a life cycle of about three years. ☐

g) Well, we like to rely on our own people. ☐

h) This time only one, in fact. However it is a very special product indeed. ☐

C **Put the words in the correct order to make questions.**

1 mean / does / What / 'launch' / ?
What does 'launch' mean?

2 like / Manager / our / talk / you / to / to / Would / Marketing / ?
....

3 a / advertising / Do / lot / on / spend / they / ?
....

4 advertise / did / range / their / they / Where / new / ?
....

5 targets / meet / Did / your / you / sales / ?
....

6 expecting / figures / sales / Were / better / you / ?
....

7 my / Have / sales / read / report / you / quarterly / ?
....

8 a / How / do / often / report / write / you / ?
....

D **Match the answers a–h to the questions in exercise C.**

a) Not yet, I'm afraid. I'll go through it first thing this afternoon.

b) Well, they do have a large budget, yes.

c) Every quarter. In the past we had to write one every month, though.

d) To make a new product available to the public.

e) Yes, that would be very useful. Thank you.

f) In all national papers and also on TV.

g) No, we are very satisfied. In fact, we've sold a lot more than we
   thought we would.

h) We certainly did.

7

WRITING

Answering enquiries

A **You work for the Marketing Department of Hamilton Food and Drink Products. You receive the following enquiry. Write a reply (100–140 words) to Mr Rijsbergen based on the notes below.**

> Dear Sir,
>
> I am interested in your range of diet products which I saw advertised in *Healthy Home*. Could you please send me a copy of your catalogue? Further details of your new brand of mineral water would also be very welcome.
>
> Many thanks.
>
> Wim Rijsbergen

Notes
thanks for enquiry / enclose catalogue / also enclose leaflet about
Fontaine, (latest brand of spring water) & say a few words about this
product (offers real benefits; recommended by medical authorities) /
offer to send representative with sample / end suitably

Reports **B** **Put the sentences a–g into the correct order to make an extract from a report. The words in bold will help you.**

a) About one-fifth of the consumers who have tried **our new products** said they were dissatisfied with the taste of the *Spring Balm* toothpaste. Also, 47 people complained of skin irritation after using our deodorant spray. ☐

b) **I shall begin with** my findings about the products themselves. ☐

c) **It** is based on information gathered from over 500 interviews with consumers. ☐

d) **On the other hand,** many of those who *have* heard about the *Spring Balm* collection complain that they cannot find our products anywhere. 7

e) **Secondly,** as regards the price, almost 90 per cent remarked that our products are overpriced in comparison with well-established brands. ☐

f) **The aim of this report** is to determine the reasons for the failure of the launch of our new range of *Spring Balm* toiletries. 1

g) **Thirdly,** with regard to promotion and place, it is clear that the name *Spring Balm* still means nothing to most consumers. ☐

C **Now complete the recommendations of the report with words from the box.**

| available | ~~basis~~ | delay | regard | retail | sure | withdrawn |

Recommendations

On the ......*basis*......¹ of the above findings, I would like to make the following recommendations.

I recommend that the deodorant spray should be temporarily ....² and submitted to laboratory tests without ....³. Our laboratory should also develop a new flavour for the toothpaste.

With ....⁴ to price, we should look carefully at our competitors' policy and make ....⁵ that our price is correct.

Finally, I suggest that we should advertise more on TV and possibly on the Internet and make sure that the *Spring Balm* collection is ....⁶ not only from a wider range of supermarkets but also from more specialised ....⁷ outlets.

Editing **D** **Read this text about successful marketing.**

In most of the lines **1–10** there is **one extra word** which does not fit. Some lines, however, are correct.

If a line is **correct**, put a tick (✓) in the space provided.

If there is **an extra word** in the line, write that word in the space provided.

The key to successful marketing consists of three broad areas. Firstly, do you need	1 ....*do*.........
to have a really passionate curiosity for the customer. So you need to be prepared	2 ....✓.........
to do a lot of hard work to get in a deep understanding of their needs, their	3 ....
behaviour and everything that really motivates for them. Secondly, you need a	4 ....
good business sense, because you want it to make some money. Obviously,	5 ....
when you are in business, one of your main goals is to make a profit because no	6 ....
business can survive if it is not profitable. Finally, you also have to have a great	7 ....
communication skills. In marketing, you have to do communicate with a lot of	8 ....
different people, such as your customers, as well as with all the other people	9 ....
involved in your projects. And it is not all about being able you to speak or write	10 ....
effectively, it is also about being a good listener.	

Planning

VOCABULARY

A **Cross out the noun which does not normally go with the verb in the bubble.**

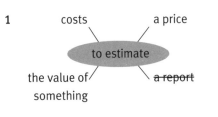

1   costs   a price
              to estimate
    the value of   a report
    something

2   sales   a profit
              to forecast
    a schedule   an increase

3   a meeting   information
              to plan
    a trip   a conference

4   a profit   research
              to do
    business   a lot of work

B **Cross out the verb which does not normally go with the noun in the bubble.**

1   to draw up   to call
              a budget
    to overspend   to stick to

2   to decrease   to stick to
              a plan
    to implement   to evaluate

3   to cancel   to implement
              a meeting
    to arrange   to reschedule

4   to finish   to submit
              a report
    to keep within to write

C **Complete each sentence with a word combination from exercise A or B.**

1   Experts ...*estimate*... the ......*value*...... of the deal at 20 million euros.

2   We have to .... the .... for Friday because the CEO is busy all day Thursday.

3   My boss is angry because I haven't quite .... my sales .... yet and she expected it last week.

4   We always .... on our products so we can prove that they are the safest on the market.

5   Our team managed to meet all the deadlines and to .... the .... that was allocated to the project.

LANGUAGE REVIEW

Talking about the future

A **These words and phrases refer to the future. Put them in order, starting with the soonest. Today is 1st June.**

a) in four days' time [ ]

b) in ten minutes [1]

c) in three weeks' time [ ]

d) next month [ ]

e) next year [ ]

f) the day after tomorrow [ ]

g) the week after next [ ]

h) tomorrow morning [ ]

i) tonight [ ]

B **Rewrite the sentences using the verbs in brackets.**

1 We are going to visit the trade fair. (*plan*)
We are planning to visit the trade fair.

2 We are sure we will make a profit within three years. (*expect*)
We expect to make a profit within three years.

3 We are going to launch a new product range next summer. (intend)

4 We will beat our competitors before long. (hope)

5 We are sure we will open three new subsidiaries next year. (expect)

6 We are going to open a new sales office in Bratislava. (*intend*)

C **Look at Florian Straub's diary for next week and study the examples. Then complete the conversation between Jessica and Florian's secretary. It is now Friday 11th.**

Mon 14th		**Fri 18th**	
a.m.	visit Bielefeld factory	**a.m.**	Geneva
p.m.	meet Korean visitors	**p.m.**	
Tues 15th		**Sat 19th**	
a.m.	9–10 give talk on word-of-mouth advertising	**a.m.**	
p.m.	prepare departmental meeting	**p.m.**	back from Geneva
Wed 16th		**Sun 20th**	
a.m.	10–11.30 departmental meeting	**a.m.**	
p.m.	to Geneva	**p.m.**	
Thurs 17th		**Notes**	
a.m.	Geneva		
p.m.			

Examples

1 *Florian Straub is visiting the Bielefeld factory on Monday morning.*

2 *On Wednesday morning, he is attending a departmental meeting.*

Jessica: Hello. I'd like to make an appointment to see Florian Straub on Wednesday afternoon.

Secretary: I'm afraid Mr Straub is ....[1] then and he's not ....[2] until Saturday.

Jessica: Right. How about Monday?

Secretary: He's tied up all day Monday. Would Tuesday suit you?

Jessica: Tuesday? Fine. What sort of time?

Secretary: Well, he's ....[3] until ten o'clock, but he could see you after that. Otherwise in the afternoon he's ....[4] but I'm sure he could fit you in.

Jessica: Three o'clock would be great.

Secretary: Three. Right. I've made a note of that. I'll call you back to confirm the appointment.

Jessica: Thank you very much.

WRITING

Linking ideas

A **Look at the examples. Then answer the questions below.**

*Our new range of cosmetics is not doing very well. **For instance**, sales of our Cleopatra day cream have fallen by 20 per cent.*

*Our competitors are already working on new designs. **That is why** we should launch our new range as soon as possible.*

*If they want to attract more tourists, they should increase the number of international flights. **In addition**, they should improve services.*

Which linker (in **bold**) is used to:

a) introduce an explanation?   ....

b) introduce an example?   ....

c) make an additional point?   ....

B **Complete the sentences with the best linker from exercise A.**

1   There are different ways you could improve your performance. *For instance*., you could try to visit five customers a day instead of three.

2   I have informed everyone personally. ...., they have all read my report.

3   I have not met my sales targets. .... I am worried I will not get a bonus.

4   I want you to meet the deadlines we agreed on. ...., I expect you to hand in your report by Thursday.

5   Prices in the city centre have gone up. .... we should look for new office space in the suburbs.

6   Montenegro is attracting more foreign investors. ...., a number of French and British companies have recently invested huge sums in the tourism industry there.

Scheduling

C **Andrea Varady is the manager of Lindcom Hungary. She is expecting three senior executives from Lindcom International Headquarters, Stockholm. Look at the schedule she has produced.**

Wednesday 24th May

11.15   Arrival Ferihegy Airport
        Transfer to Majestic Hotel
13.00   Meet all staff, Budapest Office
        Buffet Lunch, Budapest Office
15.30   Sales Team: Performance Evaluation

Thursday 25th May

08.00   Meeting with Ms Szilvia Koltai, Sales Manager
10.00   Minibus to Lindcom Electronics in Hatvan
11.00   Tour of Lindcom Electronics / Meet staff
12.00   Lunch with local manager
13.30   Return to Budapest
Free afternoon or sightseeing excursion
18.00   Airport transfer
19.45   Departure for Stockholm

Andrea receives this e-mail from Stockholm informing her about some changes. Complete the e-mail with words from the box.

~~sending~~   are leaving   cannot   has to   have to   seeing

From: Per.Jonsson@lindcom.se
To: varadyandrea@freemail.hu

Dear Andrea,
Thanks for ....*sending*....¹ the schedule.
Unfortunately, we ..*have to*....² change our plans owing to unexpected problems here at headquarters.
We ..*cannot*....³ leave on Wednesday 24th as we intended. Instead, we ..*are leaving*.. for Budapest on Thursday 25th on the same flight and returning to Stockholm on the Saturday morning.
The performance evaluation is very important. We want to have at least two full hours for that. The meeting with Ms Koltai ....*has to*..⁵ be after that, either later in the day or the day after, whichever is more convenient.
Apart from that, feel free to make any other changes you like. I apologise for the inconvenience this may cause you. Looking forward to ..*seeing*......⁶ you soon.
With best wishes,
Per

D **Write an e-mail (35–45 words) to all Sales staff.**

- Inform them of the change of time.
- Encourage everybody to be there.
- Apologise for possible inconvenience.

From: varadyandrea@freemail.hu
To: Sales staff
Subject: Visit from International Headquarters, Stockholm
Date: 16th May

Unfortunately our guests from Stockholm

Editing **E** **Read the text below about setting up a business abroad.**

In each line **1–8** there is **one wrong word**.

For each line, **underline the wrong word** in the text and **write the correct word** in the space provided.

Deciding to move abroad to set up your own business is probably one of <u>a</u>	1 ......*the*........
biggest decisions you will ever made. That is why you should plan your move	2 ....
well in advance. Firstly, it is a good idea to make several visit to the area where	3 ....
you intend to relocate. This will allow you to research your customers base, to	4 ....
assess local competition and to make usefully business contacts.	5 ....
Secondly, you could begin to learn the language of the country were you want	6 ....
to go. As the way people doing business varies from one country to another, you	7 ....
also need to learn about the culture, local costumes and business etiquette.	8 ....

LANGUAGE WORK

Managing people

VOCABULARY **A** Complete the first gap in the sentences below with a verb from Box A and the second gap with a preposition from Box B.

Box A			Box B					
believe	communicate	deal	in	in	~~to~~	to	to	with	with
delegate	invest	~~listen~~	respond						

Seven ways to manage people more successfully

1 Your staff will often have good ideas and suggestions, so ...._listen to_.... what they have to say.

2 Do not think you have to do everything yourself .... tasks .... other people.

3 Problems may be more difficult to solve if you wait too long, so .... them as soon as you can.

4 Good employees want to develop professionally, so .... courses and seminars for them.

5 Clear information is very important.................... .... your employees clearly so that they know exactly what you expect.

6 When your employees are satisfied, they work more effectively so .... their needs without delay.

7 And finally, remember that trust is essential. Your staff need a manager that they can strongly ....

B Complete the sentences with the correct prepositions.

1 Staff often complained ...... _about_ ..... the new manager, saying he didn't believe ...._in_......... their abilities.

2 Robert was arguing .... his boss .... taxation.

3 Did she talk .... you .... her plans to leave the company?

4 Good. So you all seem to agree .... me .... the main points.

5 They apologised .... everyone .... their failure to deal .... the crisis.

6 The team had to report .... their progress .... the manager every month.

C These sentences are not correct. Supply, correct or delete the prepositions as appropriate.

1 Robert never listens my suggestions.
   Robert never listens to my suggestions.

2 Socialising colleagues is sometimes a good way to learn about what is happening in different departments.

3 Linda would like to discuss about the report's recommendations with you.

4 My company spends a lot of money for training courses for employees.

5 He may become a good manager. It depends of his communication skills.

6 She told to her boss that her new job was challenging.

LANGUAGE REVIEW

Reported speech

A **Put the words in the correct order to make a reported dialogue.**

1 My / ready / wasn't / asked / my / why / me / boss / report / .
  My boss asked me why my report wasn't ready.

2 working / computer / I / my / properly / replied / wasn't / .
  ....

3 a / He / I / needed / new / one / said / that / .
  ....

4 ahead / to / Then / he / should / plan / said / try / I / .
  ....

5 organised / was / answered / well / I / usually / I / that / .
  ....

6 a / asked / computer / Finally, / get / him / I / I / new / when / would / .
  ....

B **Check your answers to exercise A. Then complete the sentences with the actual words spoken.**

1 'Why .... *isn't your report ready* ....?' asked my boss.

2 'Well, my computer ....,' I replied.

3 'I think you ....,' he said.

4 'And you should ....,' he said.

5 'But I'm ....,' I answered.

6 'When ....?' I asked finally.

C **Correct the sentences which are wrong. The first one has been done for you.**

1 He told them invest in a good training course.
  He told them to invest in a good training course.

2 She said that gaining the staff's trust is important.

3 He said me he had to deal with a lot of problems in his previous job.

4 She said I should communicate with colleagues more clearly.

5 She asked them to agree on a date for their next meeting.

6 He told that last month's sales figures were very good.

D **Look at the examples. Then report the questions below.**

Direct *wh-* questions	Reported *wh-* questions
What do you want to do?	He asked her *what* she wanted to do.
How much do you earn?	He asked her *how much* she earned.
Direct *Yes/No* questions	**Reported *Yes/No* questions**
Do you plan ahead?	He asked her *if* she planned ahead.
Could you deal with a crisis?	He asked her *if* she could deal with a crisis.

1 Do you adapt easily to new situations?
  He asked her ....

2 How often do you invest in courses?
  He asked her ....

3 Are you having difficulty contacting our consultant?
  He asked her ....

4 Why is this year's budget so small?
  He asked her ....

LANGUAGE WORK

WRITING
Reports

A Match the percentages in the box with the expressions 1–8.

| 0%   4%   31%   48%   54%   ~~73%~~   94%   100% |

1 About three-quarters of the staff .... 73% ....

2 Almost everybody / Most of the staff ....

3 Almost one-third of the staff ....

4 Everybody ....

5 Hardly anybody ....

6 Just under half of the staff ....

7 More than half of the staff ....

8 Nobody ....

B Lindcom International's managers wanted to know if their employees think they are good managers so they sent everyone a questionnaire. Look at the summary of the questionnaire findings and complete the conclusions section of the report with phrases from the box.

YOU AND YOUR MANAGER: SUMMARY OF QUESTIONNAIRE FINDINGS

		Often	Sometimes	Never
1	Does your manager listen to your suggestions?	5%	35%	60%
2	Does s/he respond to your concerns?	2%	73%	25%
3	Does s/he say 'well done'?	19%	34%	47%
4	Does s/he give you the information you need?	97%	2%	1%
5	Do you enjoy working with her/him?	33%	52%	15%

| almost everybody   almost half   ~~most of the staff~~   one-third   a quarter of |

CONCLUSIONS

.... Most of the staff ....[1] are clearly dissatisfied with the way management listens to their suggestions. In addition, ...[2] the staff say their manager never responds to their concerns. ....[3] say that they often enjoy working with their manager. On the other hand, ...[4] say that their manager never praises them. On the positive side, ...[5] is satisfied with the way their manager communicates information.

C Match the sentence halves to make the recommendations section of the report.

RECOMMENDATIONS

1 Management should build on its strengths

2 We must urgently look into ways of

3 Moreover, we should adopt

4 We should also remember to praise

5 As a result, our people would certainly enjoy

a) working with us more than they do at present.

b) and continue to communicate information efficiently.

c) our employees for their good work.

d) taking into account our employees' suggestions.

e) a more sympathetic attitude towards them.

Requesting information **D** You work for Lindcom UK. Read the course advertisement. Then complete the letter using the appropriate information (a–l).

The Morningside Business & Administration Training College

FORTHCOMING COURSES

Cultural Differences in the Workplace

The aim of this two-day workshop is to enable participants to understand cultural differences in order to improve relationships in the workplace.

Course fee: £150

Dates: to be advised

Venue: The Morningside BAT College, 13 Buccleuch Avenue, Edinburgh, EH4 7BG

Tutor: Fredrik Karlsson, MBA, PhD (Lund University)

For further details, write to Donald Strachan at the above address.

a) All the best,

b) Dear Mr Strachan

c) Hi Donald!

d) Dear Sir / Madam

e) Please write soon.

f) Sue Lowles,
    Deputy Manager Lindcom UK

g) We look forward to hearing
    from you.

h) Yours faithfully

i) Lindcom UK, 30 Burrard Street,
    Brentford, TW9 2AK

j) 11th May

k) Mr Donald Strachan
    The Morningside BAT College,
    13 Buccleuch Avenue, Edinburgh,
    EH4 7BG

l) Yours sincerely

1 *i*

2

3

4

Further to your advertisement of 7th May in *The Banffshire Herald*, we would like to request further information about your *Cultural Differences in the Workplace* course.

In particular, we would like to know the start dates and the maximum number of participants on the course.

Finally, any information about discounts for groups of five or more would also be welcome.

5

6

S Lowles

7

Conflict

VOCABULARY

A Match the sentence halves to make six tips for being a more successful negotiator.

1 Good answers don't always come quickly
2 Sometimes you have to compromise –
3 Don't get angry too quickly –
4 Don't agree with everyone all the time
5 Say when you like an idea –
6 Keep the same attitude towards others –

a) you can't be tough all the time.
b) or they'll think you're weak.
c) enthusiastic negotiators are rare!
d) be consistent.
e) so don't be too impatient.
f) try to stay calm.

B Make the adjectives negative by adding the correct prefix from the box. Use a good dictionary to help you.

| in- im- ir- un- |

1 ....*un*........sympathetic
2 ....patient
3 ....formal
4 ....responsible
5 ....cooperative
6 ....polite
7 ....responsive
8 ....emotional
9 ....critical
10 ....consistent

C Complete each sentence with the negative form of one of the adjectives a–c.

1 It was very ....*impolite*.... to be late for the meeting and not even apologise.

a) polite   b) emotional   c) formal

2 He prefers..................... meetings where everybody can relax and feel comfortable.

a) patient   b) responsive   c) formal

3 It takes two to tango. They have to try to help and stop being so ....

a) critical   b) cooperative   c) credible

4 He signed the contract without reading it. What an .... attitude!

a) responsible   b) responsive   c) emotional

5 She'll criticise you one day and praise you the next. How can anyone be so .... ?

a) patient   b) consistent   c) emotional

6 I think he is too .... He seems to accept whatever people say without thinking.

a) cooperative   b) credible   c) critical

LANGUAGE REVIEW

Conditionals

A Match the question halves.

1 Wouldn't we seem impatient
2 Will you get a bonus
3 Won't you make a concession
4 Would you increase your order
5 Wouldn't they be disappointed
6 Will Ana ever win their trust

a) if she keeps being inconsistent?
b) if they didn't win the contract?
c) if you exceed the sales target?
d) if we told them to hurry again?
e) if we delivered immediately?
f) if they make one?

B Complete Speaker B's short answers.

1 A: Would you complain if they were late?
   B: Of course ..... *I would* ....

2 A: If we placed regular orders, would they cover transport costs?
   B: No, I'm afraid ....

3 A: Perhaps they'll be less impatient if we explain our situation.
   B: Yes, I'm sure ....

4 A: They wouldn't deliver faster even if we always paid cash.
   B: .... wouldn't. They've always been terribly slow.

5 A: If she comes this morning, will you talk to their representative?
   B: .... will.

6 A: Do you think he'd resign if he didn't win the contract?
   B: No, I'm sure ....

7 A: Will you inform us if there's a delay?
   B: Yes, ...

C Complete the sentences with *'ll, 'd, won't* or *wouldn't*.

1 I'm sure they ... *wouldn't* ... continue doing business with you if they weren't satisfied.
2 If he was able to deal with pressure, he .... be an excellent negotiator.
3 If I lose this order, I'm afraid it .... affect my commission.
4 If you don't increase the discount, we .... be able to increase the size of our order.
5 We .... have to turn to another supplier if you were able to deliver this month.
6 You .... get an extra day off even if you win this contract, I'm afraid.

D Complete the sentences with the correct form of the verbs in brackets.

1 We *'ll give* .... (give) you a 15 per cent discount if you pay cash.
2 If they .... (pay) late, we'd close their account.
3 If you .... (deliver) this week, we'll place a bigger order.
4 We .... (deliver) this week if you paid cash.
5 We'll give her a free gift if she .... (increase) her order.
6 If they make a concession, we .... (do) the same.
7 If you place regular orders, we .... (cover) insurance.
8 We would consider a bigger discount if you .... (order) a larger quantity.

WRITING

Business letters

A People often start a business letter by saying why they are writing. Complete these typical opening sentences with the verbs from the box.

| complain | ~~confirm~~ | enquire | invite | request |

1 I am writing to …*confirm*…. the dates we agreed for our next meeting.

2 I would like to ………………… your advice.

3 I am writing to ……………… about the low quality of the goods you supplied.

4 I would like to ……………… you to visit our stand at the trade fair.

5 I would like to ……………… about the course advertised in the *Financial Times*.

B When you reply to a business letter, you usually begin by making reference to a previous communication. Complete the beginning of the replies to the five letters in exercise A with the words from the box.

| complaint | ~~confirming~~ | enquiry | invitation | request |

1 Thank you for …*confirming*… the dates …

2 With reference to your ……………… for advice …

3 With reference to your ……………… about the low quality …

4 Thank you for the ……………… to visit your stand …

5 With reference to your ……………… about the course …

C Put the sentences into the correct order to make an e-mail.

From:	SunSingAd@bluesky.net.au
To:	infophillips@bizcom.au
Subject:	Our order BG/503

Dear Mr Munroe

a) As we urgently need those supplies, could you please send the correct items and pick up the wrong ones as soon as possible. ☐

b) However, you sent us toner cartridges for photocopiers instead of the laser jet ones we had ordered. ☐

c) We look forward to hearing from you. ☐

d) I am writing with reference to the above order for office supplies. ☐ 1

e) In addition, three of the boxes of paper contained coloured paper. ☐

f) This morning, we ordered five toner cartridges (Ref. LXJ2) and ten boxes of white A4 photocopying paper (Ref. PA4/1). ☐

Yours sincerely

Mary Li

D Write a reply (60–75 words) to the e-mail in exercise C. The Useful language box will help you.

From:	infophillips@bizcom.au
To:	SunSingAd@bluesky.net.au
Subject:	Order BG/503

Dear Ms Li

....

....

....

Yours sincerely
Steve Munroe
Head of Customer Service

USEFUL LANGUAGE

Opening
Further to your ...
With reference to your ...
Thank you for your ...
Apologising
We would like to apologise for the problems you had.
Once again, our apologies for the inconvenience you had.

Explaining
I am afraid there was a mix-up over your order.
Promising action
The goods will be sent by special delivery.
Closing
We look forward to receiving further orders from you.
We very much hope that you will continue to do business with us.

Editing **E** Read the text below about the influence of culture on negotiating behaviour.

In each line **1–9** there is **one wrong word**.

For each line, **underline the wrong word** in the text, and write the **correct word** in the space provided.

Many people say that negotiating behaviour varies <u>for</u> one culture to another.	1	*from*
Americans, they say, is usually open, sociable and informal. For German	2	....
negotiator, on the other hand, clarity and thoroughness are crucially important,	3	....
while Spaniards are spontaneous and do not mind interrupt each other.	4	....
Of course, such generalisations may be truth to some extent, but we should be very	5	....
carefully with cultural stereotypes. To begin with, they may affect the way we	6	....
respond on other nationalities. More importantly maybe, we should remember that	7	....
each negotiator have a unique personality. We notice this more quickly when	8	....
doing business with people who come from the same country we do.	9	....

VOCABULARY

A **Read the sentences and write the missing letters to complete the adjectives.**

1 If a product is e c o n o m i c a l, it doesn't cost a lot of money to use.

2 A product that is f _ s h _ _ _ _ b _ _ is popular at a particular time.

3 An _ t t r _ c t _ _ e product is one that people find beautiful and exciting.

4 A product that is p _ p _ l _ r is enjoyed or liked by a lot people.

5 An _ f f _ c _ _ _ t product is one that you can use without wasting energy or time.

6 A product that is r _ l _ _ _ l _ can be trusted to work well.

B **Complete the sentences with words from the box.**

lasting made ~~quality~~ selling tech wearing

1 Rolex makes high-.quality.........watches.

2 Timberland makes fashionable and hard-....................boots.

3 Dell manufactures high-....................computer products.

4 Samsung has produced some best-....................mobile phones.

5 Tungsram makes long-....................light bulbs.

6 Samsonite sells practical and well-....................bags and suitcases.

C **Make new adjectives by joining a word from Box A to a word from Box B. Use the new adjectives to complete the definitions.**

Box A	Box B
custom down first multi ~~up~~	class made ~~market~~ market purpose

1 An ..upmarket.. product is expensive and usually of high quality.

2 If products are ....-....................they are made especially for one person or group of people.

3 A.................... ....product is one that has several different uses.

4 ....products are cheap and sometimes not good quality.

5 ....-....................products are of excellent quality.

D **Choose the best word (a, b or c) to complete each space in the text on page 49.**

1 a) planned   b) designed   c) sketched
2 a) fabricated   b) manufactured   c) assembled
3 a) tested   b) examined   c) researched
4 a) specifications   b) qualities   c) improvements
5 a) promoted   b) exhibited   c) displayed
6 a) discount   b) delivering   c) distribution
7 a) profitable   b) available   c) marketable
8 a) destroy   b) discontinue   c) distinguish

The life cycle of a product

All products have a life cycle. Therefore, new products are being developed all the time to replace older products which are coming to the end of their lives.

The cycle begins when a new product is ...*designed*...[1]. At that stage, there is only a plan or a drawing, which is then used when the product is ....[2]. Nobody knows how well the new product works or how good it is so it has to be....................[3]. On the basis of the test results, it may have to be modified. Once the necessary ....[4] have been made, the product is ready to be launched and then ....[5] in a number of advertising campaigns. Advertising plays a very important role and so does ....[6]. Indeed, the company has to make sure that its new product is ....[7] to as many customers as possible. Finally, when it is clear that sales are going down steadily, the company will probably decide to ....[8] the product.

LANGUAGE REVIEW

Passives

A **Match the sentence halves. Then underline the passive forms.**

1 If sales continue to fall
2 Most of the world's soccer balls are made in Asia
3 Our new computer games will be distributed
4 The existing model can be improved easily
5 The packaging will be modified
6 When Alkaphen was launched,

a) and our product will become a lot more environment friendly.
b) the competition was already testing a similar drug.
c) I'm afraid this model <u>will have to be discontinued</u>.
d) nationwide well before the advertising campaign begins.
e) so we don't have to design a new product.
f) by very young people who live in poverty.

B **Rewrite these as passive sentences. Only use *by* if it is important to say who did the action.**

1 They make Suzuki cars in Hungary, too.
   Suzuki cars are made in Hungary, too.
2 Someone is repairing your washing machine now.
3 Bayer developed this new drug.
4 They were still researching the effects of Alkaphen.
5 Bayer has retained all selling rights.
6 The question is, have we promoted our new range enough?
7 If sales continue to fall, we will have to discontinue it.
8 We should test this new product immediately.
9 We could improve its distribution.
10 We definitely have to improve the packaging.

C **Use a passive form of the verbs in the box to link the sentence beginnings (1–6) with the endings (a–f).**

do   consume   create   invent   ~~make~~   test

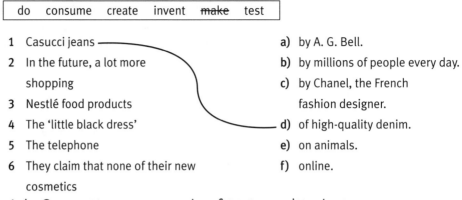

1 Casucci jeans
2 In the future, a lot more shopping
3 Nestlé food products
4 The 'little black dress'
5 The telephone
6 They claim that none of their new cosmetics

a) by A. G. Bell.
b) by millions of people every day.
c) by Chanel, the French fashion designer.
d) of high-quality denim.
e) on animals.
f) online.

1 d Casucci jeans are made of high-quality denim.

WRITING

Linking ideas

A **Study the example sentences and notice the words used to link them. Then link sentences 1–4 in a similar way.**

A fashion designer created the 'little black dress'. <u>She</u> was a genius.
The fashion designer <u>who</u> created the 'little black dress' was a genius.

A brand is a name. <u>It</u> makes it easy for customers to recognise a product.
A brand is a name <u>that/which</u> makes it easy for customers to recognise a product.

A warehouse is a large building. Goods are stored <u>there</u> until they are distributed to shops to be sold.
A warehouse is a large building <u>where</u> goods are stored until they are distributed to shops to be sold.

A recession is a period of time. The economy is doing badly <u>then</u>.
A recession is a period of time <u>when</u> the economy is doing badly.

1 This new instant coffee has been produced by a well-known company. The company has always sold its coffee in the higher price ranges.
   ....

2 The shop floor is an area in a factory. Ordinary workers do their work there.
   ....

3 A retailer is a person. She or he owns or runs a shop selling goods to members of the public.
   ....

4 Sick leave is a period of time. You stay away from your job because you are ill then.
   ....

Enquiring about a product

B **Complete the advertisement for a new product with phrases from the box.**

| further information   high-performance   including |
| market leader   run   ~~user-friendly~~ |

Just ScanIt!

At ScanIt International we put a lot of effort making our products as .....*user-friendly*.....¹ as possible. Our new scanner Alpha JTX2 continues that trend.

Alpha JTX2 will help you ....² your business smoothly and efficiently. It is a ....³ scanner designed for those who need documents in a hurry.

- Get professional results in seconds
- High-resolution scanning
- Automatic document feeder (up to 30 sheets)
- Copies up to ten pages per minute
- One-touch buttons for e-mailing images to colleagues or publishing them on a website.

Alpha JTX2: the ....⁴ in scanning technology.
Only £199, ...⁵ adaptor for slides and negatives.

For ....⁶ and a free trial, call FREEFONE 0800 427 8732 or e-mail us at scanit@hitech.co.uk

C Write an e-mail (70–90 words) to ScanIt International on behalf of your company to request further information about the scanner described in exercise B.

- Start with Dear Sir / Madam.
- Say where you saw the advertisement.
- Ask what you need to know:
  - Can the JTX2 scan 3-D objects?
  - What types of paper can be used?
- Say you are interested in a free trial and ask how long the trial period is.
- Finish your message with a suitable ending.

Editing **D** Read the text below about launching a new product.

In most of the lines **1–8** there is **one extra word** which does not fit. Some lines, however, are correct.

If a line is **correct**, put a tick (✓) in the space provided.

If there is an **extra word** in the line, write that word in the space.

Are you planning to launch a new product or service? If you are, must remember	1 .....*must*.....
that not only what you say about it is important but also *how* you say it well. You	2 ....
should try to emphasise on the features of your product which no other product	3 ....
has, i.e., its *unique selling points*. You should also try to describe them the benefits	4 ....
of your goods or services from your customers' perspective.	5 ....
Successful business and people usually know or at least have a good idea of what	6 ....
their customers want or need. This knowledge can be very useful in building	7 ....
customer satisfaction and the loyalty.	8 ....

Talk business

INTRODUCTION

The aim of this *Talk business* section is to make you more aware of some of the main features of English pronunciation. This will help you understand spoken English more easily. Hopefully, it will also help you discover areas you may need to work on for your spoken English to sound more natural.

THE SOUNDS OF ENGLISH

◄)) **1 Look, listen and repeat.**

Vowel sounds

/ɪ/	qu**i**ck f**i**x
/iː/	cl**ea**n sh**ee**t
/e/	s**e**ll w**e**ll
/æ/	b**a**d b**a**nk
/ɑː/	sm**ar**t c**ar**d
/ɒ/	t**o**p j**o**b
/ɔː/	sh**or**t c**our**se
/ʊ/	g**oo**d b**oo**ks
/uː/	sch**oo**l r**u**les
/ʌ/	m**u**ch l**u**ck
/ɜː/	f**ir**st t**er**m
/ə/	**a**ˈbout ˈCan**a**d**a**

Diphthongs

/eɪ/	pl**ay** s**a**fe
/aɪ/	m**y** pr**i**ce
/ɔɪ/	ch**oi**ce **oi**l
/aʊ/	d**ow**nt**ow**n
/əʊ/	g**o** sl**ow**
/ɪə/	n**ear** h**ere**
/eə/	f**air** sh**are**

Consonant sounds

1 Contrasting voiceless and voiced consonants

Voiceless		**Voiced**	
/p/	**p**ay	/b/	**b**uy
/f/	**f**ile	/v/	**v**alue
/t/	**t**ax	/d/	**d**eal
/θ/	**th**ink	/ð/	**th**is
/tʃ/	**ch**eap	/dʒ/	**j**ob
/s/	**s**ell	/z/	**z**ero
/k/	**c**ard	/g/	**g**ain
/ʃ/	op**ti**on	/ʒ/	deci**s**ion

2 Other consonant sounds

/m/	**m**ine	/n/	**n**et	/ŋ/	brandi**ng**	/h/	**h**igh
/l/	**l**oss	/r/	**r**ise	/w/	**w**in	/j/	**y**ear

Tips
- Identify the sounds that you have difficulty recognising or producing and focus mainly on these.
- Add your own key words in the tables above for the sounds you wish to focus on.
- Using the pause button on your CD player will give you time to speak or write when you do the exercises.

USING A DICTIONARY

Any good dictionary today gives you useful information on the pronunciation of individual words. With the help of the *Longman Business English Dictionary* or the *Longman Wordwise Dictionary*, for example, you will be able to work out the pronunciation of any English word on your own once you are familiar with the phonetic symbols above.
In addition, the dictionary also gives you essential information about *word stress*. When a word has more than one syllable, we always put more stress on one of the syllables, i.e., we speak that syllable more strongly. Look at the dictionary entry for *compete*:

com·pete /kəmˈpiːt/ *v* [I] to try to win something or to be more successful than someone else:

- The ˈ sign shows you that the syllable immediately after it should be stressed: comPETE. You will find various exercises on word stress in Units 9, 10 and 12.

- The : sign shows you that the vowel is long. The contrast between *long* and *short* vowels is very important for mutual understanding. In Unit 1, for example, you will find an exercise on /ɪ/ and /iː/, while Unit 7 has an exercise on /ɒ/ and /ɔː/.

SOUNDS AND SPELLING

In English,
a) the same sound can be spelt in different ways,
b) the same letters can be pronounced in different ways.
a) Consider for example /əʊ/, the sound of *go slow*. It can be spelt *o* as in *open*, *oa* as in *loan*, *oe* as in *toe*, *ough* as in *although*, *ow* as in *know*, or *eou* as in *Seoul*.
b) Take the letter *u* for instance. It can be pronounced /ʌ/ as in *cut*, /ʊ/ as in *full*, /ɜː/ as in *turn*, /ɔː/ as in *sure*, /juː/ as in *tune*, or /ɪ/ as in *busy*.

Put the following words under the correct sound in the table below (the letters in bold show the sound).

break	Europe	insurance	advice	train
buyer	friendship	knowledge	said	want
chair	heart	laugh	scientific	their
conscious		million		height

Vowels					
/ɒ/		/e/		/ɑː/	
1 job		1 sell		1 card	
2		2		2	
3		3		3	

/eɪ/		/eə/		/aɪ/	
1 pay		1 share		1 price	
2		2		2	
3		3		3	

Consonants					
/ʃ/		/s/		/j/	
1 option		1 sell		1 year	
2		2		2	
3		3		3	

Sound–spelling relationships are explored in Units 2, 6, 8, 9 and 10.

SHADOWING

Shadowing is a very effective way to make the most of the recorded material.
1 Play a short section, i.e. a few words or one line of a dialogue, then pause.
2 Without speaking, repeat internally what you heard.
3 Play the same section again. Pause and speak the words in exactly the same way and at the same speed. Repeat this step until you are completely satisfied with your performance.
4 Play the same section again and speak along with the voice on the recording. This is shadowing.
5 Move on to the next short section of the recording and repeat the same procedure.

Careers

INDIVIDUAL SOUNDS

A 🔊 2 **Listen to the difference between /ɪ/ and /iː/.**

/ɪ/	/iː/
Tim pick bit	team peak beat

B **Put the words from the box into the correct column, according to the pronunciation of the letter(s) in bold.**

art d**ea**ler   **e**ditor   man**a**ger   policem**a**n   t**ea**cher

/ɪ/ as in qu**i**ck f**i**x	/iː/ as in cl**ea**n sh**ee**t
....	....
....	....
	....

🔊 3 **Check your answers. Then listen and practise saying the words.**

CONNECTED SPEECH

C 🔊 4 **Listen to the pronunciation of *can* and *can't*.**

She can speak Arabic. She can't speak Greek.

She can speak Arabic but she can't speak Greek.

What's the rule?

• Within a sentence, a weak form of *can* is often used: /kən/ or /kn/.
• *can't* is usually pronounced /kɑːnt/ in British English.

D **Practise saying the sentences.**

1   He can use JavaScript but he can't use Dreamweaver.
2   She can't start this week but she can start at the end of the month.
3   I can't speak Mandarin Chinese fluently but I can understand a lot.
4   We can let you know next week but we can't promise anything.
5   She can use spreadsheets but she can't design a website.

🔊 5 **Now listen to the recording and practise saying the sentences.**

STRESS AND INTONATION

E 🔊 6 **Listen to how these questions are spoken.**

1   Can you hold?   4   Could you take a message?
2   Did you say R-E-I-T-H?   5   Could you tell me your name and address?
3   Hello. Is that John Reith?

Tip

A 'yes / no' question is usually asked with the voice going **up** at the end.

🔊 6 **Now listen again and practise saying the questions.**

SOUND WORK

TELEPHONING

A 🔊 **7 Listen and complete these phrases.**

1 Can I .....*have*..... your name, please?

2 Just one ...., please.

3 Hold ....

4 I'd .... to speak to Ms Allan.

5 I'm .... she is in a meeting just now.

6 Can I .... a message?

7 Could you ask her to call me .... this afternoon, please?

8 Could you .... me to the IT department, please?

🔊 **7 Now listen again and practise saying the sentences.**

B 🔊 **8 Listen and complete each column with the letters of the alphabet.**

/eɪ/ as in play safe	/iː/ as in clean sheet	/e/ as in sell well	/aɪ/ as in my price	/əʊ/ as in go slow	/uː/ as in school rules	/ɑː/ as in smart card
a	*b* *g*	*f*	....	....	....	....
h	*c*	*l*	....		....	
....	*d*	....			....	
....	*e*	....				

Tips

• The key words will help you remember the pronunciation of each letter of the alphabet.

• When dictating or taking down a strange word, you need to know how to pronounce each letter of the alphabet clearly and accurately.

C 🔊 **9 Listen to the extracts from phone conversations and write down the words that are spelt out.**

1 Name: ....

2 Address: ....

3 Street name: ....

4 Company name: ....

5 Name: ....

D 🔊 **10 Listen to these examples.**

	International code	Country code	Area code	Subscriber's number
1	00	Brazil: 55	São Paulo: 11	2466 5984
2	00	Turkey: 90	Istanbul: 212	613 3367

E 🔊 **11 Now listen to the extracts and write down the phone numbers.**

1 If you'd like more details, please call our Bucharest office on ....

2 And our number in Tunis is ....

3 Please contact our Montevideo subsidiary. The country code is 598 and their number is ....

4 Yes, we do have an office in Madrid. The number is .... The country code is 34, by the way, and then 91 for Madrid.

5 Our agent in Bratislava can be reached on ....

Tips

• Phone numbers are pronounced in groups. The digits are said separately.

• At the end of each group your voice goes up, except for the last group, when your voice goes down to signal that it is the end of the number.

SURVIVAL BUSINESS ENGLISH

Companies

Track 13

A ◀)) **12 Listen to how the verb forms are pronounced.**

1 syllable	deals	makes	grows
2 syllables	in·volves	re·cruits	su·pplies
3 syllables	fi·nan·ces	de·vel·ops	con·tin·ues

Track 14

INDIVIDUAL SOUNDS

Note

The symbol · is used to separate the syllables in the words.

B ◀)) **13 Listen to the recording. How many syllables do you hear?**

1	receive	2	receives	2	
2	start	1	starts	1	
3	rise	1	rises	2	
4	produce	2	produces	3	
5	deliver	3	delivers	3	
6	change	1	changes	2	

What's the rule?

If the infinitive ends in /s/, /z/, /ʃ/, ʒ/, /tʃ/ or /dʒ/, the third person singular ending of the present simple is pronounced /ɪz/ and the word gets an extra syllable.

C **Underline the forms which are one syllable longer than the infinitive. Then check your answers.**

1	move	moves	6	cost	costs
2	focus	<u>focuses</u>	7	offer	offers
3	describe	describes	8	increase	<u>increases</u>
4	catch	<u>catches</u>	9	invest	invests
5	advertise	<u>advertises</u>	10	discuss	<u>discusses</u>

◀)) **14 Now listen and practise saying the pairs of verb forms.**

CONNECTED SPEECH

Tip

We often use the weak form /ə/ when *are* appears within the sentence.

D ◀)) **15 Listen to the way *are* is pronounced in these sentences.**

1 We are looking for a reliable partner.
2 What are you doing tomorrow evening?
3 Our new chocolates are not selling well.

◀)) **15 Listen again and practise saying the sentences.**

E ◀)) **16 Listen and complete the sentences.**

1 .... a lot of business with China.
2 .... quite well this year.
3 .... good progress.
4 .... the best ice cream in the world.
5 .... a sales meeting every Friday.
6 .... a break because there's a power cut.

◀)) **16 Check your answers. Then listen again and practise saying the sentences.**

SOUND WORK

examples
/dʒ/ lodge
/ʒ/ measure
/tʃ/ church
/ʃ/ fish
/z/ criticise
/s/ lease

56

COMPANY PRESENTATIONS

A Complete the company description with words from the box.

| achieved | employ | leading | located | operate | rose |

Zengő Furniture Company Rt. (ZFC Rt.) specialises in manufacturing and retailing office furniture. Based in Pécsvárad, in the south of Hungary, we are the ....[1] Hungarian company in our field. We ....[2] eight stores ....[3] throughout the country and ....[4] 145 people altogether.

Last year, our sales ....[5] to over 40 million euros, which represents a 19 per cent increase over the previous year. Our earnings before interest and tax were 4.9 million euros, or 12 per cent of sales. This result is better than the result we ....[6] the year before, when the margin was equal to 8.7 per cent of sales.

🔊 **17 Listen to check your answers.**

B 🔊 **18 Listen to an interview with Pierre Chevrel, the General Manager of Espace Mode. Use up to three words or a number in each space to complete the fact sheet below.**

Espace Mode

COMPANY FACT SHEET

Location:	.....*Grenoble*.....[1]
Main activity:	Clothes manufacturers and ....[2]
Customers:	Men and women from all walks of life in the ....[3] 16–25. We also ....[4] to agents and mail-order catalogues.
Market position:	We are among the French ....[5] in the clothing sector.
Staff:	We employ nearly ....[6] people.
Financial information:	Annual turnover of over ....[7] million euros. Profits of ....[8] million euros, i.e., ...[9] of sales.
Future plans:	We are working on exciting new designs which reflect a completely new concept ....[10]. Espace Mode is set to become ....[11] of the European fashion market.

C Use the fact sheet in exercise B to prepare a business presentation about Espace Mode. Use the tip and the Useful language box to help you.

> **Tip**
> To present your company effectively, structure your information clearly.
> For example, you could use the headings shown in the fact sheet in exercise B.

USEFUL LANGUAGE

Introducing	Turning to a new topic	Concluding
I'd like to start by saying …	If we can now look at …	Finally, a few words about …
I'm going to talk about …	Now I'd like to turn to …	I would like to conclude by …
My main objectives are …	The next point I'd like to raise is …	Now, let me summarise the main
The aim of my presentation is to …	What I'd like to talk about now is …	points again.
The purpose of this presentation is to …		So, to sum up …
		Thank you all for your attention.

A Cross out the silent letter, i.e. the letter which is not pronounced, in each of the following words.

should	mustn't	receipt	answer	listen
foreign	know	designer	honesty	shouldn't

◀)) **19** Listen to check your answers. Check with the key. Then listen again and practise saying the words.

INDIVIDUAL SOUNDS

B Circle the word in each set where the letter(s) in bold is/are pronounced differently.

1	ret**ai**ler	p**a**yment	exch**a**nge	m**a**nufacturer
2	ref**u**nd	s**u**pplier	prod**u**ct	c**u**stomer
3	m**o**ney	**o**ffer	st**o**ck	p**o**licy
4	ret**ur**n	s**er**vice	adv**er**tise	p**ur**chase
5	cl**o**thes	c**o**mpany	neg**o**tiate	teleph**o**ne
6	rec**ei**pt	d**ea**l	p**e**riod	d**i**spatch

◀)) **20** Listen to check your answers. Check with the key. Then listen again and practise saying the words.

CONNECTED SPEECH

C ◀)) **21** Listen and complete these sentences.

1 They .... increase their order.

2 .... pay on receipt of the goods?

3 We can pay for the flat now so ....
.... worry about a bank loan.

4 Their business is quite small so .... be careful with cashflow.

5 The software was available as a download so ....
.... buy it on disc.

6 .... order some photocopying paper. We're almost out of stock.

D ◀)) **21** Listen again and check your answers. Notice how *have to* is pronounced.

What's the rule?

Have to is usually spoken as one word.
Before a vowel sound (sentences 1 and 6), it is often pronounced /ˈhæftʊ/.
Before a consonant sound (sentences 2, 3, 4 and 5), it is often pronounced /ˈhæftə/.

◀)) **21** Listen again and practise saying the sentences.

NEGOTIATING

A **Put the items a–h into the correct order to make an extract from a negotiation.**

a) Now, let's talk about how much you want to order, shall we? `1`

b) On an order of that size, and since it's your first order with us, we can offer 5 per cent but then we can offer 10 per cent off all list prices for further orders above €10,000.

c) Mm, I see. OK then. I suppose we can agree to that since you plan to put in further orders.

d) I'm sorry, we can't do that if we can't get the goods earlier. However, we can pay cash on delivery.

e) I'm afraid we can't guarantee that but we could possibly deliver by mid June. As regards payment, we would expect you to pay as soon as the goods have been shipped.

f) Right. If we buy 100 'UTec' and 150 'Supaswing' tennis rackets, what discount can you give us? `2`

g) Fine. That's it, then. I think we've covered everything.

h) All right, that sounds fair. Now, if we place an order this week, will you be able to deliver the goods within two weeks?

B **Match each item 1–5 with an appropriate response (a–e).**

1 If we order 200 units, will you give us a 10 per cent discount?

2 We would expect you to cover insurance as well.

3 We'd like you to deliver immediately.

4 We'll ship the goods by train. Is that all right?

5 You'll have to pay us in advance this time.

a) We'd rather you shipped them by road, in fact.

b) I'm sorry but that's not possible. We can only guarantee delivery within ten days.

c) Sorry but we can't agree to that. We can only cover freight.

d) Well, we'd prefer to pay you on delivery as usual.

e) I'm afraid we can only offer 5 per cent on orders of that size.

C 🔊 22 **Listen and check your answers. Then listen again and focus on the way the speakers of items a–e respond.**

> **Tip**
>
> When we give a negative answer, we do not usually say just '*No*'. Instead, we often use phrases like: '*We'd rather …*', '*I'm sorry but …*', '*Well, we'd prefer …*' and '*I'm afraid …*'. We also generally *explain* why we respond negatively.

🔊 22 **Listen again and practise saying the responses.**

SURVIVAL BUSINESS ENGLISH

Great ideas

INDIVIDUAL SOUNDS

A 🔊 **23 Listen to how these verb forms are pronounced.**

1 syllable	stopped	moved	watched
2 syllables	waited	reduced	offered
3 syllables	advertised	attracted	decided

B 🔊 **24 Listen to the recording. How many syllables do you hear?**

1	receive ....2....	received ....2....		5	launch	launched ....
2	finance	financed		6	count	counted ....
3	adapt	adapted		7	start	started ....
4	end	ended				

What's the rule?

If the infinitive of a regular verb ends in /t/ or /d/, the -ed of the past form is pronounced /ɪd/ and the verb gets an extra syllable.

C **Underline the forms which are one syllable longer than the infinitive. Then check your answers.**

1	earn	earned	5	discover	discovered	8	increase	increased
2	need	<u>needed</u>	6	ask	asked	9	invest	invested
3	describe	described	7	focus	focused	10	discuss	discussed
4	test	tested						

🔊 **25 Now listen and practise saying the pairs of verb forms.**

CONNECTED SPEECH

D 🔊 **26 Listen and complete the conversations.**

1 A: .....*Were*..... they .....*trying*..... to develop a new drug?

   B: Well, everybody thinks they were.

2 A: She .... around the world on her own.

   B: Are you sure she was?

3 A: Our competitors .... their range of products very well.

   B: Weren't they really?

4 A: The new product .... a lot of customers.

   B: Well, in fact I think it was.

5 A: He .... the next advertising campaign.

   B: Yeah and he was designing a new product at the same time.

Tip

- In positive sentences *was* and *were* are usually pronounced /wəz/ and /wə/.
- At the beginning or at the end of a sentence, *was* and *were* are often pronounced /wɒz/ and /wɜ:/.
- *wasn't* and *weren't* are always pronounced /'wɒznt/ and /wɜ:nt/.

🔊 **26 Listen again and practise saying the sentences.**

MEETINGS

A **Match the sentence halves.**

1	Hold on	a)	to the point.
2	The main aim of the meeting	b)	quite understand.
3	Sorry, I don't	c)	of a later launch date.
4	Luigi, how do you	d)	is to decide the date of the launch.
5	I'm in favour	e)	a moment.
6	Let's get back	f)	feel about this?

B 🔊 27 **Listen to eight extracts from meetings and decide what each speaker is doing.**

- Write one letter (**a–d**) next to the number of the speaker.
- Use each letter twice.

Speaker 1: ....*b*..........   a) stating the aim

Speaker 2: ....   b) changing the topic

Speaker 3: ....   c) asking for comments

Speaker 4: ....   d) summarising

Speaker 5: ....

Speaker 6: ....

Speaker 7: ....

Speaker 8: ....

C 🔊 28 **Listen to the recording and complete the extracts from meetings.**

1 Right. Let's now .....*have*..... .....*a*..... .....*look*...... at our sales figures.

2 I'm not very happy about that, ...

3 Just a minute, ...

4 .... get started?

5 Let's get .... business.

6 Well, I'm not .... that.

7 What exactly .... by 'specialist stores'?

8 I'm .... launching the product just before summer.

D **These are the opening lines of a meeting. Put them in the correct order.**

a) As you know, we're going to launch a very special new product – a unique soft drink with low sugar and carbon dioxide content.   `2`

b) Firstly, we still have to decide when exactly we should launch the product.   ☐

c) I've called this meeting for two main reasons.   ☐

d) Sania, what do you think would be the best date?   ☐

e) Secondly, we need your ideas for a new name as many of you are not very happy with the name *Vitafruit*.   ☐

f) Shall we begin?   `1`

g) So, let's turn to the launch date.   ☐

E 🔊 29 **Listen and check your answers to exercise D. Then listen again and find three differences between the recording and the text in exercise D.**

SURVIVAL BUSINESS ENGLISH

Stress

SOUND WORK

Tip

Some words have groups of two or three consonant sounds pronounced together. Such groups can be at the beginning, in the middle or at the end of words. Pronouncing those groups of consonants correctly often requires a lot of practice.

A ◀)) 30 **Listen and write the missing letters to complete the words.**

1 P r e s s u r e   _ _ o _ _ e m   _ _ o m o t i o n

2 w o r _ _ o a d   l i _ _ _ _ y l e   d e a _ _ i n e

3 c o _ _ _ a _ _ _   a _ _ _   p s y c h o l o g i _ _ _

4 He r e s i _ _ _ _ three m o _ _ _ _ ago.

5 It's a _ _ u d y about _ _ _ e s s in the w o r _ _ _ a c e.

6 She's p l a _ _ _ _ l o _ _ of p r o j e _ _ _.

◀)) 30 **Listen again and practise saying the words and sentences. Pay attention to the groups of consonants: do *not* put a vowel sound between the consonants!**

CONNECTED SPEECH

B ◀)) 31 **Listen to the pronunciation of *has / have* and *hasn't / haven't* in the sentences.**

1 /z/   She's completely changed her lifestyle.

2 /ˈhæznt/   He hasn't seen a stress counsellor yet.

3 /v/   They've appointed a new management team.

4 /ˈhævnt/   They haven't introduced flexitime yet.

C ◀)) 32 **Listen to the recording and complete the sentences.**

1 .... never made a presentation.

2 .... never travelled abroad.

3 .... gone on a training course.

4 .... been under a lot of stress.

5 .... taken time off work this year.

6 .... finished our report.

◀)) 32 **Listen again and practise saying the sentences. Pay attention to the contractions.**

STRESS AND INTONATION

D ◀)) 33 **Listen and complete the question tags in the sentences.**

1 They were overworked, ... they?

2 She's been under stress recently, ... she?

3 They weren't feeling relaxed, ... they?

4 You haven't missed the deadline, ... you?

5 He resigned last week, ... he?

6 She didn't come to work yesterday, ... she?

Tip

In spoken English, you can use a question tag if you expect someone to agree with you. When you use such question tags, your voice goes down: He hasn't finished yet, has he?

◀)) 33 **Listen again and practise saying the sentences.**

MAKING AND RESPONDING TO SUGGESTIONS

A 🔊 34 **Listen and complete Speaker B's suggestions.**

a) B: ....*How* ....*about* ...... introducing flexitime?

b) B: .... asking your boss to stop putting them up?

c) B: .... call a meeting to discuss the problem so we can look for ways of making them less strict?

d) B: .... make sure they don't have to work overtime more than once a week.

e) B: .... carry out a survey to find out how many people would go to a gym.

f) B: Well, ... you take it home with you and finish it over the weekend, then.

g) B: .... hire someone part-time if he can't manage alone?

B **Match Speaker A's problems (1–7) with the suggestions (a–g) in exercise A.**

1 A: Employees who leave early have become a serious problem. ☐ *a*

2 A: There's always a long queue at the reception desk. I don't think Peter can cope on his own. ☐

3 A: Our admin staff all say they can't balance their work and home lives because of the longer hours. ☐

4 A: I'm afraid I can't finish this report by Friday. ☐

5 A: I don't think I'm the only one who's interested in keeping fit. ☐

6 A: I can't meet my sales targets. ☐

7 A: Everybody complains about the tight deadlines. ☐

C 🔊 35 **Listen to suggestions (1–8) and match them with the responses (a–h) below.**

a) Excellent idea! We could offer a full month after they've been with us for over three years. ☐

b) Mm, good idea. Most of our employees have children. I'm sure they'd welcome the idea. ☐

c) Yes, I suppose that's worth considering. We'd certainly have a longer weekend! ☐ *1*

d) Maybe, but I think sending out a questionnaire would be more effective. ☐

e) I'm not sure I agree. In my view, we should keep at least one smoking area somewhere. ☐

f) I'm afraid that's out of the question. We can't afford to take on a psychologist. ☐

g) I don't agree at all. They already have free membership of the sports centre. ☐

h) That sounds interesting but I think varying the menus and offering healthier meals is more important. ☐

SURVIVAL BUSINESS ENGLISH

Entertaining

INDIVIDUAL SOUNDS

A Circle the word in each group where the letter(s) in bold is/are pronounced differently.

1	crab	lamb	(water)	salmon
2	entert**ai**nment	veget**a**bles	b**a**ked	st**ea**k
3	**o**nion	br**o**ccoli	l**o**bster	b**o**ttled
4	dess**er**t	s**er**vice	t**ur**key	atmosph**ere**
5	m**e**dium	sw**ee**t	v**ea**l	health**y**
6	st**ar**ter	s**a**lty	dr**au**ght	ch**ar**ge

◀)) 36 **Check your answers. Then listen and practise saying the words.**

CONNECTED SPEECH

B ◀)) 37 **Listen to how *for*, *of*, *at* and *from* are pronounced.**

1	A: You've bought some chocolates. Who are they for?	/fɔː/
	B: I bought them for you!	/fə/
2	A: What's it made of?	/ɒv/
	B: I think it's made of wood.	/əv/
3	A: What are they looking at?	/æt/
	B: I think they're looking at you!	/ət/
4	A: Where was he from?	/frɒm/
	B: They say he was from Iceland.	/frəm/
5	A: I wonder if this is the train to Brussels or from Brussels.	/frɒm/
	B: Sorry, no idea!	

What's the rule?

Many prepositions have two different pronunciations – a strong form and a weak form. We normally use the weak form (see Speaker B in conversations 1–4) but, if the preposition is at the end of the sentence (Speaker A in conversations 1–4), we use the strong form. We also use a strong form when we want to show a contrast (Speaker A in conversation 5).

◀)) 37 **Listen again and practise the conversations.**

What's the rule?

When a word finishes with a consonant sound and the word immediately after begins with a vowel sound, we usually link those two words.

C ◀)) 38 **Listen to the way certain words are linked in these sentences.**

1 She put‿off the meeting.
2 She put‿it‿off.
3 I looked‿up their‿address.
4 I looked‿it‿up.

◀)) 38 **Now listen again and practise saying the sentences.**

D **Indicate where similar links could be made in these sentences.**

1 Several extra visitors turned up.
2 They took up our invitation.
3 She took us out to an excellent restaurant.
4 Jim took part in an unusual event.
5 We should set up online sales as soon as we can.

◀)) 39 **Check your answers. Then listen and practise saying the sentences.**

MAKING SMALL TALK

A **Complete the extracts from conversations with words from the box. You will not need all the words.**

| afraid | can | did | do | ~~have~~ | how | know | like | meet |
| nice | please | see | thank | thanks | what | would |

1 A: David, ...*have*....... you met Elisa Vasconcelos?
  B: No. Hello, Elisa. Nice to .... you.

2 A: Jameel, do you .... Sylvia?
  B: Yes, of course. Hi Sylvia, good to .... you again.

3 A: How do you .... ? My name's Ralph Karsten.
  B: .... to meet you. Mine's Brendan Lenihan.

4 A: .... are things?
  B: Fine .... It's good to be here.

5 A: .... I get you something to drink?
  B: That .... be nice, thanks. I'll have some fruit juice.

◀)) **40 Listen and check. Then listen again and practise speaker B's part.**

B ◀)) **41 Listen and tick the most appropriate response a), b) or c) for each item that you hear.**

1 a) How about you?
  b) Yeah. Just a little delay.   ✓
  c) Yes. I'm on the first flight to Paris tomorrow.

2 a) It's great. And just a five-minute walk from here.
  b) It's 502 2798.
  c) Yes. There are two excellent hotels in the Old Town.

3 a) Never again, thank you very much.
  b) Well, I never.
  c) Just once. I attended a conference here two years ago.

4 a) Yes, please.
  b) Help yourself to some food.
  c) As long as I stick to the city centre, I'm fine.

5 a) Till the end of the conference.
  b) At the Palace Hotel.
  c) Yes, quite a long time, in fact.

6 a) Sure. It's 233 2453.
  b) Yes, of course. Just go ahead.
  c) E-mailing is much faster.

C ◀)) **42 Listen to conversation openings (1–7) and match them to the responses (a–g).**

a) Did you? Were you based in Kuala Lumpur? ☐
b) Mm. Is that one of the martial arts? ☐
c) So do you work in a laboratory? ☐
d) What a coincidence! And what sort of music does she like? ☐
e) You must be exhausted! Why didn't you fly? [1]
f) Really! That's one of the largest cities in Poland, isn't it? ☐
g) I'm glad you like it! And what's your favourite dish? ☐

Tip

Responding with just one or two words is not usually enough for a successful conversation. To show interest and keep the conversation going, make a comment or ask a question related to the topic, as in examples in exercise C.

SURVIVAL BUSINESS ENGLISH

New business

INDIVIDUAL SOUNDS

A 🔊 **43 Listen to the difference between /ɒ/ and /ɔː/.**

/ɒ/ as in top job	/ɔː/ as in short course
not spot wok	nought sport walk

B **Underline all the letters that are pronounced /ɔː/ in these sentences.**

1 We'll send them all on a training course.
2 Let's sort out this problem before Pauline gets here.
3 According to this report, interest rates will soon fall.
4 We need to reform our tax system in order to stimulate exports.
5 They've closed forty of their stores and cut their workforce by a quarter.

🔊 **44 Listen and check your answers. Then listen again and practise saying the sentences.**

> **Tip**
> To improve your pronunciation, getting the difference between long and short vowels is one of the most important things. So, make sure your long vowels are really long! (See also Unit 1, exercises A and B.)

STRESS AND INTONATION

C 🔊 **45 Listen to how these dates are spoken. Notice the main stresses in bold.**

1 15th June   the **fif**teenth of **June** (BrE)
2 June 15th   **June** fif**teenth** (AmE)

> **Tip**
> In British English, you usually say and write the day first, followed by the month. In American English, it is usually the other way round: month first, followed by the day. In American English, you do not need to say *the* before the ordinal.
> When you write the date, you can leave out the ending *-st /-nd /-rd /-th*, e.g. 16 March.

D **Write the dates in full.**

1 14 May ....   3 16 April............................
2 Sept. 15............................   4 Dec. 17............................

🔊 **46 Listen and check your answers. Then listen again and underline the two stressed syllables you hear in each date.**

E **Say these dates out loud.**

1 20 February   4 July 30, 2010   7 12 October 1999
2 February 20   5 23 May 1990   8 3 November
3 30th August 2008   6 January 13, 2003

🔊 **47 Listen and check. Then listen again and practise saying the dates.**

NUMBERS **A** 🔊 **48 Listen to the recording and circle the number you hear.**

1	(£13)	£30	5	$18,000	$80,000
2	14%	40%	6	€1,200	€12,000
3	350 million	315 million	7	2/5	2.5
4	¥1,416	¥1,460	8	1.47	1.74

🔊 **48 Listen again and practise saying the numbers.**

Practice other fractions ½ ⅔ ¾ ⅚ ⅛ ¹⁄₁₆ ¹⁄₃₂

B **Match the questions (1–6) with the answers (a–f).**

1 Did the unemployment rate decrease?

2 Do you know the latest Footsie index[1]?

3 What's the basic rate of income tax in the UK?

4 And what percentage of all income taxpayers pay the basic rate? *o*

5 What's the euro–dollar exchange rate?

6 What's the population of the UK?

o a) About 75 or 80 per cent, I think.

b) Hold on … . Yes. It closed 114.2 points higher at 5,833.9 points.

c) Mm, I'm not sure but I think one euro is about 1.3 US dollars. Hold on, I'll check.

d) Mm, just over 62 million, I'd say. So that's over 250 people per square kilometre.

e) Well, I guess it must be around about 20 per cent.

f) Yes. It went down by 0.5 per cent to reach 7.9 per cent.

[1]Footsie index: the Financial Times Stock Exchange 100 Index – the main measure of the amount by which the leading 100 shares sold on the London Stock Exchange have gone up or down in value. It is updated once every minute of the working day.

🔊 **49 Listen and check your answers. Then listen again and practise saying the sentences.**

C 🔊 **50 Listen to the economic profile and complete the summary with the numbers you hear.**

THE COUNTRY IN FIGURES

Growth rate:	3.1 %	**Labour force**	2.967 million	**Budget**		
GDP per capita:	$ 26,200	Services:	81 %	Revenues:	$ 54.7 billion	
Inflation rate:	2.3 %	Industry:	14 %	Expenditure:	$ 53.1 billion	
		Agriculture:	5 %			
		Unemployment rate:	4.9 %			

D 🔊 **51 Listen to how Speaker B corrects Speaker A.**

1 A: Was that 2.5 per cent?   B: No. 2.8 per cent.

2 A: Did you say 2.4 per cent?   B: Sorry, no. 3.4 per cent.

E **Read these conversations and underline the numbers that Speaker B will stress.**

1 A: So the unemployment rate went up by 1.2 per cent.

B: Sorry, no, it was 1.1 per cent.

2 A: So, 36.7 per cent of the people in Denmark own a computer.

B: 37.7 per cent, to be precise.

3 A: Did you say the GDP totalled £853 billion last year?

B: Not quite. I said £843 billion.

🔊 **52 Listen and check. Then listen again and practise Speaker B's part.**

Marketing

INDIVIDUAL SOUNDS

A ◀)) 53 Listen to how the letters in bold are pronounced.

> a**v**ailable pla**c**e **m**arketing **a**dvert wan**t** percen**tage**

B Write the words from exercise A next to the key phrase which contains the same sound (see page 52).

1 /ə/ as in a**b**out Ca**n**ada <u>*available*</u>   4 /ɪ/ as in qui**ck** fix ....

2 /æ/ as in **b**ad **b**ank ....   5 /ɑː/ as in **sm**art **c**ard ....

3 /eɪ/ as in **pl**ay **s**afe ....   6 /ɒ/ as in **t**op **j**ob ....

C Put the words in the box in the correct column, according to the pronunciation of the letter(s) in bold.

> ad**va**ntage be**ha**viour **ca**mpaign **co**mpany **co**rporate **fa**vourite **fo**recast
> i**m**age **qua**lity **ta**rget **th**anks **wa**sn't

/ə/ as in about Canada	/æ/ as in bad bank	/eɪ/ as in play safe	/ɪ/ as in quick fix	/ɑː/ as in smart card	/ɒ/ as in top job
....	....	....	*advantage*	....	....
....	....	....	....	....	....

◀)) 54 Listen and check. Listen again and practise saying the words.

CONNECTED SPEECH

D ◀)) 55 Listen to how the words in *italics* are pronounced in these questions from a customer survey.

1 Which age group *do you* belong to?

2 How much *did you* spend on soft drinks last month?

3 *Would you* consider buying a different brand?

> **Tip**
>
> In informal speech, *do you* is often pronounced /djə/ or /djʊ/. *Did you* and *Would you* are often pronounced /ˈdidjə/ or /ˈdidjʊ/ and /ˈwʊdjə/ or /ˈwʊdjʊ/.

◀)) 55 Listen again and practise asking the questions.

E ◀)) 56 Listen to the recording and complete the questions.

1 .... take the packaging into account?

2 How often .... buy spring water?

3 How many bottles of water .... buy last week?

4 .... try fruit-flavoured mineral water?

5 What kind of soft drinks .... usually buy?

◀)) 56 Listen again and practise asking the questions.

USING STRESS TO CORRECT INFORMATION

A ◀)) **57 Listen to these telephone conversations. Notice how Speaker B uses stress to correct Speaker A.**

1 A: ... and your agent in Uruguay is Juan José Buaro. B-U-A-R-O ...

   B: Sorry, no. B-U-<u>E</u>-R-O.

2 A: All right. See you on Tuesday, then.

   B: Hold on a minute. The meeting is on <u>Thurs</u>day.

B **Look at the telephone conversations. Underline the part that Speaker B will stress to correct Speaker A.**

1 A: Ah, hello Miss Peterson.

   B: Hello Mr Gallegos, it's <u>Mrs</u> Peterson, actually. How can I help you?

2 A: ... and my sales report will be with you by the thirtieth.

   B: Sorry, Ranesh. We're talking about the thirteenth.

3 A: So their number is 020 8224 7895.

   B: No, 8224 6895.

4 A: ... and you said the advertising agency was at 75 Birchington Street.

   B: Well, it's Birchington Road, actually.

5 A: I hear you increased your market share by 9.5 per cent.

   B: Sorry, I said 5.5 per cent.

6 A: And you said 40 per cent of the people you interviewed had difficulty finding our products.

   B: That's not quite right. I said 14 per cent.

◀)) **58 Listen and check. Listen again and practise Speaker B's replies.**

GETTING THE MESSAGE RIGHT

C ◀)) **59 Listen to how Speaker B asks for the unclear piece of information to be repeated.**

1 A: We interviewed more than ***** people.

   B: Sorry, how many people did you interview?

2 A: ***** is unhappy about our sales figures.

   B: The line's very bad, I'm afraid. Who's unhappy about our sales figures?

D **Ask Speaker B to repeat the missing information in each of these statements.**

1 A: So our new hair conditioner will be launched on *****.

   B: I couldn't hear you. ....?

2 A: We've already spent ***** on advertising.

   B: Sorry, ...?

3 A: The ***** Manager was really very pleased.

   B: Sorry, ...?

4 A: He'd like to meet you on ***** in the afternoon.

   B: It's a very bad line. ....?

5 A: Our new range of toiletries should be targeted at *****.

   B: Sorry, ...?

6 A: Our total sales were over *****.

   B: Sorry, ...?

◀)) **60 Now listen to the sample answers and practise Speaker B's responses.**

SURVIVAL BUSINESS ENGLISH

Planning

INDIVIDUAL SOUNDS

A 🔊 61 **Listen to how the letters in bold are pronounced.**

h**o**liday d**o** inf**or**mation **or**dinary **o**ther **o**verspend w**or**k

B **Put the words from exercise A in the correct column, according to the pronunciation of the letters in bold.**

/ɒ/ as in t**o**p j**o**b	/ɔː/ as in sh**or**t c**our**se	/uː/ as in sch**oo**l rules	/ʌ/ as in m**u**ch l**u**ck
holiday			

/ɜː/ as in f**ir**st t**er**m	/ə/ as in **a**bout Can**a**da	/əʊ/ as in g**o** sl**ow**

C **Put the words from the box in the correct column in exercise B, according to the pronunciation of the letters in bold.**

c**o**mpany f**ore**cast m**o**ve **o**ffice **o**pen peri**o**d w**or**ld

🔊 62 **Check your answers. Then listen and practise saying the words.**

CONNECTED SPEECH

D 🔊 63 **Listen to the pronunciation of *to* in these sentences.**

1 They expect to make a huge profit.
2 They are going to relaunch the series very soon.
3 They are hoping to attract foreign investors.

> **What's the rule?**
> Before a consonant sound (sentences 1 and 2), *to* is often pronounced /tə/.
> Before a vowel sound (sentence 3), *to* is often pronounced /tʊ/.

E **Say these sentences.**

1 What are you going to do?
2 They intend to expand in Poland.
3 He is planning to take early retirement.
4 We're hoping to open a subsidiary in Madrid.
5 They're going to do some research on their new product.

🔊 64 **Listen to the recording and practise saying the sentences.**

STRESS AND INTONATION

F **For each verb, write the corresponding noun ending in *-tion* or *-sion*.**

1	inf<u>orm</u>	*information*	5	celebrate	....	9	modernise	....
2	implement	....	6	renovate	....	10	discuss	....
3	prepare	....	7	expand	....	11	decide	....
4	consider	....	8	expect	....	12	revise	....

🔊 65 **Listen to the recording and underline the stressed syllable in each verb and noun. Listen again and practise saying the words.**

MEETINGS **A** 🔊 66 **Listen to six extracts from meetings and decide what the female speaker is doing in each case. Write one letter, a), b) or c), next to the number of the extract. Use each letter twice.**

Extract 1: .... b ....   a) dealing with an interruption

Extract 2: ....   b) interrupting

Extract 3: ....   c) requesting a clarification

Extract 4: ....

Extract 5: ....

Extract 6: ....

CHECKING INFORMATION **B** **Match the statements (1–6) with the appropriate request for clarification (a–f).**

1 A: We forecast an increase in sales.

2 A: I don't think I can finish my report by Wednesday.

3 A: Unfortunately, they didn't estimate the costs properly.

4 A: I hope Peterson will attend the board meeting.

5 A: They're not expecting to move into their new offices until January.

6 A: It seems that there's going to be a slight delay.

a) B: You mean, it was a lot more expensive?

b) B: So what you're saying is that they are not sticking to their plan.

c) B: What exactly do you mean by 'slight delay'?

d) B: Are you saying that business is picking up, then?

e) B: You mean, you're not completely sure he'll come?

f) B: So what you're saying is that you won't be able to meet the deadline.

🔊 67 **Listen to the recording to check your answers. Then listen again and practise Speaker B's responses.**

C **A secretary from Lindcom Hungary is calling Szilvia, the Sales Manager. Complete the conversation with the sentences from the box.**

Kati: Szilvia?

Szilvia: .... Yes. Speaking. ....¹

Kati: Hi. I'm phoning about our visitors from Stockholm. I'm afraid they've changed their plans.

Szilvia: ....²

Kati: Yes, they are. But they're arriving on Thursday, not on Wednesday as they originally planned.

Szilvia: ....³

Kati: Well, I think they're going to be very busy all day Thursday. You know, the performance evaluations and all that. They could see you after that but I'm sure Friday morning would be better. Would 10 o'clock be convenient for you?

Szilvia: ....⁴

Kati: How about earlier, say 8.30?

Szilvia: ....⁵

Kati: Fine. I'll confirm the appointment as soon as possible.

Szilvia: ....⁶

a) I see. So what about our meeting?

b) All right. Let's make it 8 o'clock, just to be on the safe side.

c) Well, I'm seeing an important client at 10.15. I can't change that, I'm afraid.

d) Thanks, Kati. That's great.

e) ~~Yes. Speaking.~~

f) You mean, they're not coming next week?

🔊 68 **Listen and check your answers.**

D **Underline all the forms in exercise C which are used to talk about the future.**

INDIVIDUAL SOUNDS

A **Make four groups of words with the same sounds.**

training	approach	persuasive	goal	number
order	other	report	shareholder	talk	trust	pay

1 sales   *training*   ....
2 launch   ....
3 money   ....
4 flow   ....

🔊 **69 Listen to the recording to check your answers. Then listen again and practise saying the words.**

CONNECTED SPEECH

B 🔊 **70 Listen to the way certain words are linked in these sentences.**

1 They told every one of us.
2 She finds it easy to delegate authority.
3 He believes in his employees' abilities.
4 They've invested a lot in training courses.
5 She likes to communicate information as often as possible.

What's the rule?

When a word finishes with a **consonant** sound and the word immediately after begins with a **vowel** sound, we usually link those two words.

🔊 **70 Listen again and practise saying the sentences.**

C **Show where similar links could be made in these sentences.**

1 He gained a lot of experience abroad.
2 She told us that Alan wouldn't agree.
3 The department isn't investing enough in training.

🔊 **71 Listen to the recording and check your answers. Then listen again and practise saying the sentences.**

STRESS AND INTONATION

D **Put the words from the box in the correct column, according to their stress pattern.**

assistant	consultant	deputy	invoice	manager	support

O o	o O	O o o	o O o
budget	mistake	shareholder	suggestion
....	....	....	....
		....	....

🔊 **72 Listen and check. Then listen again and practice saying the words.**

SOCIALISING

A **Complete the sentences used when people say goodbye.**

1 Keep .... in .... touch.

2 We'll .... in touch soon.

3 .... a safe journey back.

4 I hope we'll see you .... soon.

5 Thanks for looking .... me so well.

6 Thanks ever so much .... your hospitality.

🔊 **73 Listen and check your answers.**

B **Match the questions (1–6) with the appropriate replies (a–f).**

1 What do you usually do after work?

2 Any plans for this evening?

3 What do people here usually do at weekends?

4 We're going out. Why don't you join us?

5 How do you usually spend the summer?

6 So what do you think of Copenhagen?

a) It's great. Thanks for showing me around.

b) That's very kind of you but some other time.

c) Well, I'd just like to stay in the hotel and relax.

d) We all go to see my parents in Toulouse.

e) Not much. I sometimes watch a DVD.

f) Many people go to their holiday cottages in the hills.

🔊 **74 Listen and check your answers. Then listen again and practise saying the responses.**

C 🔊 **75 Tick the most appropriate response a), b), or c) to each item that you hear.**

1 a) I really enjoyed the meal.

b) I hope we meet again soon. It's been great to be here. ✓

c) People always say that to me.

2 a) That was really hard work, wasn't it?

b) I've enjoyed it too. Thank you.

c) Yes, I like pleasure too.

3 a) Goodbye! Keep in touch!

b) And even better to you.

c) No, you're the best.

4 a) Not at all. Now it's your turn to invite us.

b) Many happy returns!

c) You're welcome. It's been great to have you with us.

5 a) It's very kind of you but perhaps some other time.

b) It's Saturday afternoon already.

c) Thanks. Same to you.

TAKING A MESSAGE

D 🔊 **76 Your colleague Jim is away and has asked you to check his voice mail. Listen to the four messages. Note down who rang and what was said or asked. Then write a short note for your colleague. The first one has been done for you.**

Max called about your presentation on Friday. He asked what time you wanted to start. He also asked if the boardroom was OK.

INDIVIDUAL SOUNDS

Tip

Notice that non-stressed syllables often have a schwa sound (/ə/).

A ◀)) 77 Listen to the *schwa* sound (/ə/) in these words (see page 52).

O o	o O	o O o	O o o
pati**e**nt	pr**o**pose	behavi**ou**r	compr**o**mise
nerv**ou**s	s**u**ccess	c**o**nsistent	symp**a**thy

◀)) 77 Listen again and practise saying the words.

B In each word, underline the letter(s) pronounced /ə/.

1 advice 3 company 5 customer
2 solution 4 complaint 6 entertainment

◀)) 78 Listen to the recording and check your answers. Then listen again and practise saying the words.

CONNECTED SPEECH

C ◀)) 79 Listen to how the forms in bold are spoken.

1 We **won't** pay. 4 We**'d** complain. 7 She**'ll** send it.
2 We**'ll** see. 5 I**'ll** do it. 8 She**'d** sign it.
3 We **wouldn't** answer. 6 I**'d** agree.

D ◀)) 80 Listen and complete the sentences with *'ll, won't, 'd,* or *wouldn't*.

1 I .'d............ resign immediately.
2 I.................... send them a fax.
3 We.................... deliver the goods this week.
4 They.................... close our account.
5 We.................... reduce the price.
6 We.................... pay all transport costs.
7 They.................... pay you a higher commission.
8 We.................... sign the contract.

◀)) 80 Listen and check. Listen again and practise saying the sentences.

STRESS AND INTONATION

Tip

Notice the rising intonation at the end of the first part of the sentence and the falling intonation at the end of the second part.

E ◀)) 81 As you listen to the recording, match the sentences halves.

↗	↘
1 If we pay late,	a) they'll give you a bonus.
2 If you delivered this week,	b) we'll give you an extra discount.
3 If you gave us a 10 per cent discount,	c) they'll close our account.
4 If you exceed the sales target,	d) we'd pay all transport costs.
5 If you pay cash,	e) we'd place our order early next week.

◀)) 81 Listen again and practise saying the sentences.

DEALING WITH CONFLICT

A ◀)) 82 **Listen to five different people talking about various conflict situations. Decide what the conflict was about.**

- Write one letter (**a–g**) next to the number of the speaker.
- Do not use any letter more than once.

Speaker 1: ...._e_..........	a) a misunderstanding about a deadline
Speaker 2:	b) a personality clash between colleagues
Speaker 3:	c) a team leader unhappy about the schedule
Speaker 4:	d) an e-mail sent to the wrong person
Speaker 5:	e) a buyer and a seller disagreeing about some of the terms of a deal
	f) staff and manager unable to work together
	g) staff unhappy about extra administrative work

B ◀)) 82 **Listen again and decide what the consequence of each conflict was.**

- Write one letter, **a) – g)**, next to the number of the speaker.
- Do not use any letter more than once.

Speaker 1: ...._f_..........	a) nobody agreed to work part-time
Speaker 2:	b) the company decided to employ more staff
Speaker 3:	c) the employee asked to work in a different group
Speaker 4:	d) the manager left the company
Speaker 5:	e) somebody apologised
	f) the company cancelled the order
	g) some employees resigned

C ◀)) 83 **Listen and complete the telephone conversation.**

A: Phillip's Office Supplies International. Good morning.

B: It's Mary Li here, from Sun Sing Advertising.

A: Hello, Ms Li. How can I........_help_........ ....?

B: I'd like to make a complaint.

A: What seems to.................... ....?

B: You have just sent us the wrong invoice, I'm afraid.

A: Can you give me the details, please.

B: Right. The invoice number is 202A and the order number you quote is BG/505. In fact, our order number is BG/503.

A: Now, let me see. I'm.................... .... It's our fault entirely. I'm afraid there's been a mix-up.

B: When do you think you.................... sort.................... ....?

A: I'll.................... .... and call you back as soon as possible.

B: Thank you.

A: Don't.................... .... Goodbye Ms Li.

◀)) 83 **Listen again and practise Speaker B's part.**

SOUND WORK

A 🔊 **84 Listen and write the missing letters to complete the words.**

1 S̲t̲ylish   _ _ o w   _ _ o d u c e

2 c o _ _ _ _ _ a b l e   m a n u f a _ _ u r e

3 Our new _ _ o d u _ _ _ are a _ _ _ a _ _ i v e and _ _ a _ _ i c a l.

4 They're also _ _ e x i _ _ _ and user-_ _ i e n _ _ y.

5 _ _'_ d e s i _ _ _ _ for c u _ _ o m e r s with busy l i _ _ _ _ y l e s.

6 They h a _ _ _'_ a n n o u _ _ _ _ the l a u _ _ _ date yet.

> **Tip**
>
> Some words have groups of two or three consonant sounds pronounced together. Such groups can be at the beginning, in the middle or at the end of words. Pronouncing those groups of consonants correctly often requires a lot of practice.

🔊 **84 Listen again and practise saying the words and sentences. Pay attention to the groups of consonants.**

CONNECTED SPEECH

B **Complete the sentences with *Its*, *It has* or *It is*.**

1 ...... It is .... ideal for storing CDs.

2 .... got lots of interesting features.

3 .... weight is just under 3 kilos.

4 .... most attractive feature is that .... easy to operate.

5 .... got all you need for home and office use.

6 .... available in three different colours.

🔊 **85 Check your answers. Then listen and practise saying the sentences. Use the contractions (e.g., it's), as in the recording.**

STRESS AND INTONATION

C 🔊 **86 Listen and complete items 1–8.**

1 .... It's .... delivered ...   5 .... advertised ...

2 .... manufactured ...   6 .... promoted ...

3 .... modified ...   7 .... tested ...

4 .... discontinued ...   8 .... insured ...

🔊 **86 Listen again and practise saying items 1–8.**

Tips

- Notice the contractions, e.g., *they have been* is pronounced /ðeɪvbɪn/, etc.
- Notice the weak forms, e.g., /ə/ for *are*, /wə/ for *were*, etc.
- Notice also the stress on the verbs, e.g., de*li*vered, discon*tin*ued, etc.

D **Match the sentence endings (a–h) with the items (1–8) from exercise C.**

a) ... after the tests.   [ ]   e) ... because of poor sales.   [ ]

b) ... against fire.   [ ]   f) ... in Korea.   [ ]

c) ... in all the national newspapers. [ ] g) ... in our laboratories.   [ ]

d) ... extensively.   [ ]   h) ... within a week.   [1]

🔊 **86 Check your answers. Then listen again and practise saying the sentences.**

ASKING QUESTIONS ABOUT A PRODUCT

A 🔊 **87 Listen and tick the most appropriate response, a), b), or c), for each item that you hear.**

1 a) Yes, I could.
   b) Well, we are expert furniture makers.
   c) Sure. To start with, it's made of the finest wood. ✓

2 a) It comes in three shades of brown, each with a matt or gloss finish.
   b) I'm afraid it's not available this year.
   c) It's got a very attractive colour and it's great value for money.

3 a) The special screen gives excellent images.
   b) Without the battery it's just under 250g.
   c) As I said, you can hold it in the palm of your hand.

4 a) No, I said it did.
   b) Yes. It is the most economical on the market.
   c) As you can see, it's ideal for travelling.

5 a) I agree. Absolutely unique.
   b) It will be sold everywhere.
   c) Its small size and its beautiful design.

6 a) There's a 12-month basic guarantee on all our products.
   b) Of course. We always do.
   c) Everything is still under guarantee.

PRESENTING A PRODUCT

B **Complete the text with words from the box.**

advantage	appeal	costs	~~features~~	ideal	length	steel	stylish
value	weighs						

> Our new model has several special ...*features*.... which will
> .... to our customers.
> * It's .... and it's made of stainless ....
> * It .... just under 2.2 kilos and its .... is 21 centimetres.
> * It's .... for the office.
> * Another .... is that it's very user-friendly.
> * And finally, it .... 99 euros – great .... for money!

🔊 **88 Listen to the presentation and check your answers.**

C 🔊 **89 Listen to extracts from six presentations. Match the extracts to the products a–f.**

a) a burglar alarm ☐
b) a coffee machine ☐ *1*
c) an executive briefcase ☐
d) a printer ☐
e) an air-conditioner ☐
f) a watch ☐

77

Answer key

LANGUAGE WORK

1 Careers

Vocabulary

A

2 b   3 a   4 b   5 a   6 c
7 c   8 a   9 a   10 c

B

2 looks
3 deals
4 is responsible
5 makes sure
6 is in charge

C

2 with   3 after   4 that   5 for

Language review

A

2 let
3 moving
4 start
5 contact
6 sharing
7 send

B

b 4   c 5   d 7   e 6   f 1   g 2

C

1 could
2 was able to
3 could
4 was able to
5 was able to

Writing

A

2 Telephone
3 E-mail
4 Profile
5 Achievements
6 Special skills
7 Experience
8 Qualifications
9 Personal details
10 Interests
11 Referees

B

2 Achievements
3 Special skills
4 Interests
5 Profile

C Sample answer

> Dear Sir or Madam,
>
> With reference to your advertisement in *The Hastings Herald* of 25th June, I would like to apply for the position of Communications Assistant.
>
> I feel I am well qualified for the position as I have A levels in Social Sciences and Literature. As for my personal qualities, I am outgoing and like meeting new people.
>
> Please let me know if you require any further information.
>
> I look forward to hearing from you.
>
> Yours faithfully,
>
> [your name]

D

2 employs *not* employ
3 keep *not* keeping
4 than *not* then
5 questions *not* question
6 in *not* for

2 Companies

Vocabulary

A

2 at   8 in
3 of   9 on
4 by   10 at
5 to   11 in
6 at   12 for
7 of

B

2 d   3 b   4 c   5 a   6 g   7 f

C

2 self-employed
3 supplies
4 parent
5 subsidiary
6 head office
7 service
8 workforce

Language review

A

2 a   3 c   4 b   5 f   6 d

B

1 What *are you doing* on Friday morning?
5 Our company *is looking* for a new Sales Manager.
6 At the moment, we *do not know* the profit figures.

C

2 has
3 travels *or* goes
4 is going *or* is travelling
5 speaks
6 is attending
7 is thinking
8 knows
9 is preparing

D Sample answers

2 How many countries does Kayavis have distributors in?
3 When is Leandra going to Canada?
4 Why is she going to Canada?
5 What foreign languages does she speak?
6 Why is she learning German? / Why is she attending a German course?
7 Where is the owner of Kayavis thinking of opening a shop and a large restaurant?

Writing

A

a 4   b 7   c 5   d 2
e 1   f 6   g 3   h 8

B Sample answer

From:	Rik_Barneveld@ntlworld.nl
To:	supersound@ntlworld.com
Subject: 14th June meeting	

Hi Ya Ling,
Thanks for the draft agenda of our forthcoming meeting. It seems fine to me. However, I think we should also discuss setting up online sales. Increasing sales and profits is extremely important for our company and going online is probably the best way to achieve that.
I too look forward very much to seeing you soon.
Kind regards,
Rik

C

3 ✓
4 ✓
5 them *not* they
6 ✓
7 attaching *not* attach
8 suggestions *not* suggestion
9 ✓
10 apologies *not* apologise

D

2 but
3 but
4 so
5 because
6 but
7 so
8 because
9 so
10 because

3 Selling

Vocabulary

Across		Down	
1	bargain	2	retailer
6	guarantee	3	purchase
7	stock	4	refund
8	bulk	5	dispatch
9	read	10	order
12	details	11	mall
13	wholesaler		

Language review

A

1 b   2 c   3 d   4 a

B

2 should dispatch orders quickly
3 you don't have to
4 shouldn't talk a lot about yourself
5 don't have to pay until August
6 mustn't make any mistakes
7 must have

C

2 d   3 e   4 a   5 f   6 b

D

Past: didn't have to; had to
Present: don't have to; have to
Future: 'll have to; won't have to

Writing

A

2 10
3 155
4 50
5 5
6 T-shirts
7 83.23
8 1,581.27
9 Tim Atkinson
10 Edinburgh

B

2 receipt
3 deliver
4 hesitate
5 doing

C

1 Dear
2 Thank you
3 We confirm
4 goods
5 We look forward to doing
6 Yours sincerely

D

3 a
4 ✓
5 they
6 to
7 and
8 ✓
9 to

4 Great ideas

Vocabulary

A

2 made a breakthrough
3 protecting the environment
4 takes advantage of
5 wins an award
6 extend our range
7 meets a need

B

2 make
3 reduce
4 raise
5 do
6 get

Language review

A

2 d   3 e   4 f   5 b   6 a

B

2 At first, the agency *did not believe* that the machine would save so much time.
4 The story goes that Professor Auenberg *had* the idea for the electric shoebrush while he was washing up.
7 Zirkon *was already making* good profits when it introduced its new digital camera in 2010.

C

1 was losing; launched; went up; improved
2 were having; phoned; wanted
3 were planning; waited; was selling
4 decided; was working; was touring; developed; took; believed

Writing

A

b 3   c 6   d 5   e 4   f 2

B Sample answer

On Sunday, the International Exhibition is open from 10 a.m. to 6 p.m.
The admission charge for groups of 10 or more is 8 francs per person.
The official catalogue is published in French, German and English only.

C Sample answer

To:	Montse Balaguer
Re:	Document shredder
Date:	7th May

Dear Montse,
At the International Exhibition of Inventions, New Techniques and Products last Sunday I saw a new type of confidential document shredder which I think would save us a lot of time and money.
The machine shreds both paper and cardboard and is fully automatic. It is also very quiet.
I think it would be a very good investment as it would be more economical in the long run than using the services of a specialist firm.
You can get more information from their website on www.safe-shreds.com.
Regards,
[your name]

D

3 the
4 ✓
5 was
6 they
7 and
8 never
9 ✓
10 for

5 Stress

Vocabulary

A

2 a   3 b   4 b   5 a   6 c   7 c   8 a
9 b   10 b   11 b

B

1 in; to
2 for; about
3 of; in
4 of; to
5 at; for
6 to; of

Language review

A

3 Yes, she has.
4 No, she hasn't.
5 No, they haven't.
6 Yes, they have.
7 Yes, Sergio has.

B Sample answers

3 Has Yaling ever dealt with an aggressive customer?
4 Has Heinrich ever dealt with an aggressive customer?
5 Have Heinrich and Ahmed ever taken part in a conference call?
6 Has Yaling ever taken part in a conference call?

C

2 's been *or* has been
3 haven't had *or* have not had
4 expected
5 thought
6 have been
7 had to
8 was
9 offered
10 needed
11 saved
12 've worked *or* have worked
13 've never felt *or* have never felt

Writing

A Sample answer

According to a recent survey(,) over 14 per cent of all employed people in the EU suffer from stress. Two of the main reasons are overwork and fear of redundancy. In addition, a large number of employees are suffering from headaches, backache and chest pains because of overcrowded offices, poor ventilation and badly designed furniture and equipment. Over the last few years this has resulted in increased levels of absenteeism and a gradual decrease in productivity.

B

2 a) However, more men than women suffer from stress-related illnesses.
  b) That is because their coping strategies are not as good as women's.
3 a) These pressures come from home and from work.
  b) By contrast, many men are only under pressure at work.
4 a) To begin with, women are much more flexible than men.
  b) Also, they usually cope with the pressures better than men.

C

The order is: 1, 4, 3, 2

D

b) showed; increased   4
c) have made *or* are making   6
d) have risen   2
e) has fallen; stand   5
f) went up; stands   3

E Sample answer

To: Slawa Kowalska
From: [your name]

I'm very sorry I won't be able to attend the seminar tomorrow morning. I need to stay at home for a couple of days because I can't shake off these terrible headaches. Moreover, I feel exhausted because I haven't slept well for a whole week.
These are probably symptoms of stress so I will see my doctor and perhaps a stress counsellor as well.
I'll be back in my office on Wednesday morning.

F

2 absence *not* absent
3 are *not* is
4 leads *not* leading
5 better *not* best
6 general *not* generally

6 Entertaining

Vocabulary

A

2 recommended
3 cosy
4 delicious
5 efficient
6 book
7 guest
8 relax
9 aperitif
10 menu
11 variety
12 dishes
13 order
14 starter
15 course
16 negotiate
17 dessert
18 bill
19 cash
20 Marketing

B

2 c   3 c   4 b   5 a

C

2 *bottled* should be crossed out;
  all the other words are methods of cooking.
3 *excellent* should be crossed out;
  all the other words describe how meat (e.g. steak) is cooked.
4 *draught* should be crossed out;
  all the other words are used to describe food or a dish.

Language review

A

2 b   3 f   4 g   5 h   6 d   7 e   8 a

B

The order is: 1, 5, 2, 7, 6, 8, 4, 3
An alternative order is: 1, 5, 2, 7, 6, 3, 8, 4

C

2 set up
3 put (it) off
4 turn down
5 gave up
6 carrying out
7 hold on; put (you) through
8 came up with

Writing

A

2 The most popular activity
3 Secondly
4 almost as many
5 far less frequently
6 with a very small number
7 Finally

B

2 c   3 a   4 e   5 b

C Sample answer

To:	Jim.Byrne@lycos.com
From:	BMarks@easynet.co.uk

Dear Jim,
We've booked Robert Dorey into the Astoria for two nights (5th and 6th).
He will be in Room 507, which is on a non-smoking floor.
The Astoria is a very comfortable four-star hotel just five minutes from the centre.
Looking forward to Robert's visit.
Best wishes,
Brian

D Sample answer

To:	BMarks@easynet.co.uk
From:	robdorey@lycos.com

Dear Brian(,)
This is to thank you for your hospitality during and after the conference.
You gave me a lot of your time and made my visit very memorable. Walking round the old town in the evening was really fascinating. Also(,) I thought the food in that Mediterranean restaurant where we had supper was just perfect.
It was a great pleasure to meet you. If you come to Canada, I would like to return your kindness and generosity.
Once again, thank you.
Regards(,)
Robert

7 New business

Vocabulary

A

2   unemployment rate
3   exchange rate
4   labour force
5   government bureaucracy
6   gross domestic product
7   balance of trade
8   inflation rate
9   foreign investment
10 tax incentives

B

2 a   3 f   4 e   5 d   6 c

C

1   subsidies
2   foreign debt
3   recession

Language review

A

4   We'll phone you when the goods are here.
7   We'll deal with insurance after they've told us about their special discount.
8   Our guests would like to visit the production unit before they go back to Qatar.

B

2 d   3 b   4 a   5 c   6 g   7 e

C Sample answers

2   I want to see Julia's report as soon as she's finished it. (or ... as soon as she finishes it.)
3   I won't invite them until they've apologised. (or ... until they apologise.)
4   Let's contact his referees before we employ him.
5   I'll give you a copy of the report when I've typed it up.
6   Read the contracts when you're on the plane.
7   Let's buy now before prices increase.
8   As soon as we win the contract, we'll inform our shareholders. (or As soon as we've won the contract, ...)

Writing

A

2 e   3 f   4 c   5 b   6 a

B Sample answers

2   The government is making exports easier in order to improve the balance of trade.
3   In order to stop companies polluting the air and the water, the government is passing a very strict environmental law.
4   The government is raising taxes in order to reduce the budget deficit.
5   In order to stimulate consumer spending, the government is lowering the interest rate.
6   The government is reducing bureaucracy in order to attract foreign investors.

C

A third of all men employed were in manufacturing in 2000, compared with only a *quarter* in 2010.
On the other hand, around one in *six* men employed were in health, education and public administration services in 2000, while the same industry accounted for one-fifth of men's jobs in 2010.
As regards the percentage of men employed in financial and business services, it increased from *10* per cent in 2000 to 15 per cent *ten* years later.

D Sample answer

One-fifth of all women employed were in manufacturing in 2000, compared with only one-tenth a decade later.
On the other hand, 40 per cent of women employed were in health, education and public administration services in 2000, while this sector accounted for 45 per cent of women employed ten years later.
As regards the percentage of women employed in financial and business services, it doubled from 2000 to 2010, when it accounted for one-fifth of women employed.

E

3	an	9	✓
4	and	10	so
5	their	11	but
6	the	12	✓
7	✓	13	it
8	so		

8 Marketing

Vocabulary

A

Across		Down	
1	share	2	agency
5	free	3	range
6	need	4	budget
7	cycle	5	figures
9	aim	8	costs
10	sales	9	ads
11	sell		

B

2 a   3 b   4 b   5 c   6 a   7 c   8 c

Language review

A

2 Why
3 How much
4 How many
5 Who
6 Which
7 How long
8 What

B

b 8   c 1   d 6   e 5   f 7   g 2   h 4

C

2 Would you like to talk to our Marketing Manager?
3 Do they spend a lot on advertising?
4 Where did they advertise their new range?
5 Did you meet your sales targets?
6 Were you expecting better sales figures?
7 Have you read my quarterly sales report?
8 How often do you write a report?

D

b 3   c 8   d 1   e 2   f 4   g 6   h 5

Writing

A Sample answer

> Dear Mr Rijsbergen,
>
> Many thanks for your enquiry of 2nd June.
>
> Please find enclosed our current catalogue, which contains detailed information about all our healthy food and drink products.
>
> We also enclose a leaflet about *Fontaine*, our leading brand of spring water. *Fontaine* is a lightly sparkling natural spring water with no calories which offers real benefits. We are particularly proud that the medical authorities of our country have already recommended it for consumption in hospitals and school restaurants.
>
> Please let us know if you would like one of our representatives to visit you and present you with a sample of all our best-selling soft drinks.
>
> We look forward to hearing from you.
>
> With best wishes,
>
> [your name]

B

a 4   b 3   c 2   d 7   e 5   f 1   g 6

C

2 withdrawn
3 delay
4 regard
5 sure
6 available
7 retail

D

3 in
4 for
5 it
6 ✓
7 a
8 do
9 ✓
10 you

9 Planning

Vocabulary

A

2 *a schedule* should be crossed out
3 *information* should be crossed out
4 *a profit* should be crossed out

B

2 *to decrease* should be crossed out
3 *to implement* should be crossed out
4 *to keep within* should be crossed out

C

2 reschedule (the) meeting
3 finished (my sales) report
4 do research
5 stick to (the) budget

Language review

A

a 5   b 1   c 7   d 8   e 9
f 4   g 6   h 3   i 2

B

3 We intend to launch a new product range next summer.
4 We hope to beat our competitors before long.
5 We expect to open three new subsidiaries next year.
6 We intend to open a new sales office in Bratislava.

C Sample answers

1 leaving for Geneva
2 coming back
3 giving a talk
4 preparing for a meeting

Writing

A

a That is why
b For instance
c In addition

B

2 In addition
3 That is why
4 In addition *or* For instance
5 That is why
6 For instance

C

2 have to
3 cannot
4 are leaving
5 has to
6 seeing

D Sample answer

From: varadyandrea@freemail.hu
To: Sales staff
Subject: Visit from International Headquarters,
         Stockholm
Date: 16th May

Unfortunately our guests from Stockholm cannot be with
us on Wednesday 24th. So the performance evaluation is
on Thursday 10.30–12.30. *False (they won't have arrived yet)*
I expect all members of the Sales team to be there.
I'm sorry if these changes cause you any inconvenience.

E

2 make *not* made
3 visits *not* visit
4 customer *not* customers
5 useful *not* usefully
6 where *not* were
7 do *not* doing
8 customs *not* costumes

10 Managing people

Vocabulary

A

2 delegate (tasks) to
3 deal with
4 invest in
5 Communicate with
6 respond to
7 believe in

B

2 with; about
3 to; about
4 with; on
5 to; for; with
6 on; to

C

2 Socialising <u>with</u> colleagues is sometimes a
   good way to learn about what is happening in
   different departments.
3 Linda would like to discuss ~~about~~ the report's
   recommendations with you.
4 My company spends a lot of money <u>on</u> training
   courses for employees.
5 He may become a good manager. It depends <u>on</u> his
   communication skills.
6 She told ~~to~~ her boss that her new job was challenging.

Language review

A

2 I replied my computer wasn't working properly.
3 He said that I needed a new one.
4 Then he said I should try to plan ahead.
5 I answered that I was usually well organised.
6 Finally, I asked him when I would get a new computer.

B

2 isn't working properly
3 need a new one
4 try to plan ahead
5 usually well organised
6 will I get a new computer

C

3 He *told* me he had to deal with a lot of problems in his
   previous job. *or* He said *that* he had to deal with a lot
   of problems in his previous job.
6 He *said* that last month's sales figures were very
   good. *or* He told *me* (*him* /*her* /*us*, etc.) that last
   month's sales figures were very good.

Note: The second sentence (She said that gaining the
staff's trust *is* important.) is correct because when we
report something that is still true, we do not need to
change the verb. However it is also correct to change the
verb into the past: She said that gaining the staff's trust
was important.

D

1 if she adapted easily to new situations.
2 how often she invested in courses.
3 if she was having difficulty contacting their consultant.
4 why this year's budget was so small

Writing

A

2	94%		6	48%
3	31%		7	54%
4	100%		8	0%
5	4%			

B

2	a quarter of		4	almost half
3	One-third		5	almost everybody

C

2 d   3 e   4 c   5 a

D

2 k   3 j   4 b   5 g   6 l   7 f

11 Conflict

Vocabulary

A

2 a   3 f   4 b   5 c   6 d

B

2 impatient
3 informal
4 irresponsible
5 uncooperative
6 impolite
7 unresponsive
8 unemotional
9 uncritical
10 inconsistent

C

2 informal
3 uncooperative
4 irresponsible
5 inconsistent
6 uncritical

Language review

A

2 c   3 f   4 e   5 b   6 a

B

2 they wouldn't
3 they will
4 No, they
5 (Yes,) I will
6 he wouldn't
7 we (or I) will

C

2 'd   5 wouldn't
3 'll   6 won't
4 won't

D

2 paid
3 deliver
4 would deliver or 'd deliver
5 increases
6 will do or 'll do
7 will cover or 'll cover
8 ordered

Writing

A

2 request
3 complain
4 invite
5 enquire

B

2 request
3 complaint
4 invitation
5 enquiry

C

a 5   b 3   c 6   d 1   e 4   f 2

D Sample answer

> From: infophillips@bizcom.au
> To: SunSingAd@bluesky.net.au
> Subject: Order BG/503

> Dear Ms Li
> Further to your e-mail of 23rd March, we would like to apologise for the problems you had.
> There was obviously a mix-up over your order and the goods you received were meant for another customer. The correct order was sent by special delivery and should already be with you.
> Once again, our apologies for this inconvenience.
> We look forward to further orders from you.
> Yours sincerely
> Steve Munroe
> Head of Customer Service

E

2 are *not* is
3 negotiators *not* negotiator
4 interrupting *not* interrupt
5 true *not* truth
6 careful *not* carefully
7 to *not* on
8 has *not* have
9 as *not* like

12 Products

Vocabulary

A

2 fashionable
3 attractive
4 popular
5 efficient
6 reliable

B

2 hard-wearing
3 high-tech
4 best-selling
5 long-lasting
6 well-made

C

2 custom-made
3 multipurpose
4 Downmarket
5 First-class

D

2 b   3 a   4 c   5 a   6 c   7 b   8 b

Language review

A

2 f; are made
3 d; will be distributed
4 e; can be improved
5 a; will be modified
6 b; was launched

B

2 Your washing machine is being repaired now.
3 This new drug was developed by Bayer.
4 The effects of Alkaphen were still being researched.
5 All selling rights have been retained by Bayer.
6 The question is, has our new range been promoted enough?
7 If sales continue to fall, it will have to be discontinued.
8 This new product should be tested immediately.
9 Its distribution could be improved.
10 The packaging definitely has to be improved.

C

2 f; In the future, a lot more shopping will be done online.
3 b; Nestlé food products are consumed by millions of people every day.
4 c; The 'little black dress' was created by Chanel, the French fashion designer.
5 a; The telephone was invented by A. G. Bell.
6 e; They claim that none of their new cosmetics are (or have been) tested on animals.

Writing

A

1 This new instant coffee has been produced by a well-known company *which* (or *that*) has always sold its coffee in the higher price ranges.
2 The shop floor is an area in a factory *where* ordinary workers do their work.
3 A retailer is a person *who* owns or runs a shop selling goods to members of the public.
4 Sick leave is a period of time *when* you stay away from your job because you are ill.

B

2 run	5 including
3 high-performance	6 further information
4 market leader	

C Sample answer

From:
To: scanit@hitech.co.uk
Subject: Request for information about the Alpha JTX2

Dear Sir / Madam,
With reference to your advertisement in the September issue of *TechNews*, we would like to request further information about the Alpha JTX2.
In particular, we need to know whether it can scan 3-D objects and also what types of paper it takes.
We are considering asking for a free trial. Could you tell us how long we would be able to keep the machine?
Thank you in advance.
Looking forward to hearing from you.
Yours faithfully,
[your name]

D

2 well	6 and
3 on	7 ✓
4 them	8 the
5 ✓	

TALK BUSINESS

Introduction

Vowels		
/ɒ/	/e/	/ɑː/
1 job	1 sell	1 card
2 knowledge	2 friendship	2 heart
3 want	3 said	3 laugh

/eɪ/	/eə/	/aɪ/
1 pay	1 share	1 price
2 break	2 chair	2 buyer
3 train	3 their	3 height

Consonants		
/ʃ/	/s/	/j/
1 option	1 sell	1 year
2 conscious	2 advice	2 Europe
3 insurance	3 scientific	3 million

1 Careers

Sound work

B *See audio script 3.*

Survival business English

A *See audio script 7.*

B *See audio script 8.*

C *See audio script 9.*

E *See audio script 11.*

2 Companies

Sound work

B

2 start:	1 syllable	starts:	1 syllable
3 rise:	1 syllable	rises:	2 syllables
4 produce:	2 syllables	produces:	3 syllables
5 deliver:	3 syllables	delivers:	3 syllables
6 change:	1 syllable	changes:	2 syllables

C *See audio script 14.*

E *See audio script 16.*

Survival business English

A *See audio script 17.*

B

2 retailers
3 age range
4 supply wholesale products
5 top three
6 300
7 190
8 7.6
9 4 per cent
10 in teenage fashion
11 the leader

3 Selling

Sound work

A

~~shoul~~d mus~~t~~n't recei~~p~~t answ~~er~~ lis~~t~~en
forei~~g~~n ~~k~~now desi~~g~~ner ~~h~~onesty shou~~l~~dn't

B

2 supplier
3 m**o**ney
4 adv**er**tise
5 c**o**mpany
6 di**s**patch

C See audio script 21.

Survival business English

A

a 1   b 3   c 7   d 6
e 5   f 2   g 8   h 4

B

2 c   3 b   4 a   5 d

4 Great ideas

Sound work

B

2	finance:	2 syllables	financed:	2 syllables
3	adapt:	2 syllables	adapted:	3 syllables
4	end:	1 syllable	ended:	2 syllables
5	launch:	1 syllable	launched:	1 syllable
6	count:	1 syllable	counted:	2 syllables
7	start:	1 syllable	started:	2 syllables

C See audio script 25.

D See audio script 26.

Survival business English

A

2 d   3 b   4 f   5 c   6 a

B

Speaker 2: a
Speaker 3: d
Speaker 4: c
Speaker 5: b
Speaker 6: d
Speaker 7: c
Speaker 8: a

C See audio script 28.

D

a 2   b 4   c 3   d 7   e 5   f 1   g 6

E

1 a major new product / a very special new product
2 have to agree / have to decide
3 are not satisfied / are not very happy

5 Stress

Sound work

A See audio script 30.

C See audio script 32.

D See audio script 33.

Survival business English

A See audio script 34.

B

2 g   3 d   4 f   5 e   6 b   7 c

C

a 7   b 3   c 1   d 2
e 4   f 8   g 6   h 5

6 Entertaining

Sound work

A

2 vegetables
3 onion
4 atmosphere
5 healthy
6 salty

D See audio script 39.

Survival business English

A See audio script 40.

B

2 a   3 c   4 c   5 a   6 b

C

a 6   b 4   c 5   d 3   e 1   f 7   g 2

7 New business

Sound work

B See audio script 44.

D See audio script 46.

E See audio script 47.

Survival business English

A See audio script 48.

B

2 b   3 e   4 a   5 c   6 d

C See audio script 50.

E See audio script 52.

8 Marketing

Sound work

B

2 <u>a</u>dvert
3 pl<u>a</u>ce
4 percent<u>ag</u>e
5 m<u>a</u>rketing
6 w<u>a</u>nt

C *See audio script 54.*

E *See audio script 56.*

Survival business English

B *See audio script 58.*

D *See audio script 60.*

9 Planning

Sound work

B *See audio script 63.*

C *See audio script 63.*

F *See audio script 65.*

Survival business English

A

Extract 2: a
Extract 3: c
Extract 4: c
Extract 5: a
Extract 6: b

B

| 2 f | 3 a | 4 e | 5 b | 6 c |

C

| 2 f | 3 a | 4 c | 5 b | 6 a |

D *See audio script 68.*

10 Managing people

Sound work

A *See audio script 69.*

C *See audio script 71.*

D *See audio script 73.*

Survival business English

A *See audio script 73.*

B

| 2 c | 3 f | 4 b | 5 d | 6 a |

C

| 2 b | 3 a | 4 c | 5 c |

D Sample answers

2 Sue Short from Datatrax phoned about your order number AB/987. She said they didn't have Item 14 in stock. She asked if they could send you another model of the same quality.

3 Phil from Human Resources phoned about next week's job interviews. He asked how many candidates you wanted to interview. He also asked if you needed any help.

4 Yeliz Gumus rang about your visit to Izmir. She said she'd booked you into the Crowne Plaza Hotel. She asked if you could send her your flight details.

11 Conflict

Sound work

B *See audio script 78.*

D *See audio script 80.*

E

| 1 c | 2 d | 3 e | 4 a | 5 b |

Survival business English

A

Speaker 2: f
Speaker 3: a
Speaker 4: g
Speaker 5: b

B

Speaker 2: g
Speaker 3: e
Speaker 4: b
Speaker 5: c

C *See audio script 83.*

12 Products

Sound work

A *See audio script 84.*

B

2 It has
3 Its
4 Its; it is
5 It has
6 It is

C

1 It's (It is) de<u>li</u>vered
2 They're (They are) manu<u>fac</u>tured
3 It was <u>mo</u>dified
4 They were discon<u>tin</u>ued
5 It's (It has) been <u>ad</u>vertised
6 They've (They have) been pro<u>mo</u>ted
7 It'll (It will) be <u>tes</u>ted
8 They'll (They will) be in<u>sured</u>

D

| a 3 | b 8 | c 5 | d 6 | e 4 | f 2 | g 7 |

Survival business English

A

| 2 a | 3 b | 4 b | 5 c | 6 a |

B *See audio script 88.*

C

| a 5 | b 1 | c 6 | d 3 | e 2 | f 4 |

Audio scripts

Introduction

1

The sounds of English
Vowel sounds

/ɪ/	quick fix
/iː/	clean sheet
/e/	sell well
/æ/	bad bank
/ɑː/	smart card
/ɒ/	top job
/ɔː/	short course
/ʊ/	good books
/uː/	school rules
/ʌ/	much luck
/ɜː/	first term
/ə/	a'bout 'Canada

Diphthongs

/eɪ/	play safe
/aɪ/	my price
/ɔɪ/	choice oil
/aʊ/	downtown
/əʊ/	go slow
/ɪə/	near here
/eə/	fair share

Consonant sounds
1 Contrasting voiceless and voiced consonants

Voiceless		Voiced	
/p/	pay	/b/	buy
/f/	file	/v/	value
/t/	tax	/d/	deal
/θ/	think	/ð/	this
/tʃ/	cheap	/dʒ/	job
/s/	sell	/z/	zero
/k/	card	/g/	gain
/ʃ/	option	/ʒ/	decision

2 Other consonant sounds

/m/	mine
/n/	net
/ŋ/	branding
/h/	high
/l/	loss
/r/	rise
/w/	win
/j/	year

2
Tim; team
pick; peak
bit; beat

3
/ɪ/ as in quick fix: editor; manager
/iː/ as in clean sheet: art dealer; policeman; teacher

4
She can speak Arabic. She can't speak Greek.
She can speak Arabic but she can't speak Greek.

5
1 He can use JavaScript but he can't use Dreamweaver.
2 She can't start this week but she can start at the end of the month.
3 I can't speak Mandarin Chinese fluently but I can understand a lot.
4 We can let you know next week but we can't promise anything.
5 She can use spreadsheets but she can't design a website.

6
1 Can you hold?
2 Did you say R-E-I-T-H?
3 Hello. Is that John Reith?
4 Could you take a message?
5 Could you tell me your name and address?

7
1 Can I have your name, please?
2 Just one moment, please.
3 Hold on.
4 I'd like to speak to Ms Allan.
5 I'm afraid she is in a meeting just now.
6 Can I take a message?
7 Could you ask her to call me back this afternoon, please?
8 Could you transfer me to the IT department, please?

8
/eɪ/ as in play safe: a; h; j; k
/iː/ as in clean sheet: b; c; d; e; g; p; t; v
/e/ as in sell well: f; l; m; n; s; x; z
/aɪ/ as in my price: i; y
/əʊ/ as in go slow: o
/uː/ as in school rules: q; u; w
/ɑː/ as in smart card: r

9
1 Hello. My name's Glen Strachan. That's S-T-R-A-C-H-A-N.
2 The address is 47, Buccleuch Square, Edinburgh. I'll spell that for you: B-U-C-C-L-E-U-C-H.
3 So I'll go over the name of the street again: El Falaky. That's E-L, new word, F-A-L-A-K-Y, number 52, Cairo.
4 I work for de Vuyst Consultants in Brussels. That's small D-E new word V-U-Y-S-T. Got that?
5 Miyako? Sure. M-I-Y-A-K-O.

10
1 00 55 11 2466 5984
2 00 90 212 613 3367

11
1 If you'd like more details, please call our Bucharest office on 00 40 1 3322 040.
2 And our number in Tunis is 216 1 768 009.
3 Please contact our Montevideo subsidiary. The country code is 598 and their number is 2 600 5467.
4 Yes, we do have an office in Madrid. The number is 328 67 53. The country code is 34, by the way, and then 91 for Madrid.
5 Our agent in Bratislava can be reached on 421 7 753 0886.

12
1 syllable: deals; makes; grows
2 syllables: involves; recruits; supplies
3 syllables: finances; develops; continues

13
1   receive; receives
2   start; starts
3   rise; rises
4   produce; produces
5   deliver; delivers
6   change; changes

14
1   move; moves
2   focus; <u>focuses</u>
3   describe; describes
4   catch; <u>catches</u>
5   advertise; <u>advertises</u>
6   cost; costs
7   offer; offers
8   increase; <u>increases</u>
9   invest; invests
10 discuss; <u>discusses</u>

15
1   We are looking for a reliable partner.
2   What are you doing tomorrow evening?
3   Our new chocolates are not selling well.

16
1   We do a lot of business with China.
2   We're doing quite well this year.
3   They're making good progress.
4   They make the best ice cream in the world.
5   She has a sales meeting every Friday.
6   She's having a break because there's a power cut.

17
Zengő Furniture Company Rt. (ZFC Rt.) specialises in manufacturing and retailing office furniture. Based in Pécsvárad, in the south of Hungary, we are the leading Hungarian company in our field. We operate eight stores located throughout the country and employ 145 people altogether.
Last year, our sales rose to over 40 million euros, which represents a 19 per cent increase over the previous year. Our earnings before interest and tax were 4.9 million euros, or 12 per cent of sales. This result is better than the result we achieved the year before, when the margin was equal to 8.7 per cent of sales.

18
Interviewer: So, Mr Chevrel, your company is called *Espace Mode*. Is that how you say it?
Pierre: That's right, yes. Exactly.
Interviewer: Where are you based and what exactly do you do?
Pierre: We are situated in Grenoble and we are manufacturers and retailers of clothes under the 'C-Kool' and 'Mirabelle' brand names.
Interviewer: Who are your customers?
Pierre: Young men and women from all walks of life in the age range 16 to 25. People who want to feel good and look beautiful! We also supply wholesale products to agents and mail-order catalogues.
Interviewer: What is the current position of your company and how many people do you employ?
Pierre: Well, we are among the French top three in the clothing sector. As regards our workforce, we employ almost 300 people.
Interviewer: Now that we are on to figures, would you like to give us some financial information?
Pierre: Certainly. Last year, we achieved an annual turnover of over 190 million euros and generated profits of 7.6 million, that is to say 4 per cent of sales.
Interviewer: Finally, how about the future?
Pierre: We are working on exciting new designs which will reflect a completely new concept in teenage fashion. I'm sure this will make *Espace Mode* the leader of the European fashion market.
Interviewer: We are certainly looking forward to seeing those new designs. Thank you very much, Mr Chevrel. We now come to the end of our business programme …

19
should; mustn't; receipt; answer; listen
foreign; know; designer; honesty; shouldn't

20
1   ret**ai**ler; p**ay**ment; exch**a**nge; m**a**nufacturer
2   ref**u**nd; s**u**pplier; pr**o**duct; c**u**stomer
3   m**o**ney; **o**ffer; st**o**ck; p**o**licy
4   ret**ur**n; s**e**rvice; adv**e**rtise; p**ur**chase
5   cl**o**thes; c**o**mpany; neg**o**tiate; teleph**o**ne
6   rec**ei**pt; d**ea**l; p**e**riod; d**i**spatch

21
1   They won't have to increase their order.
2   Do I have to pay on receipt of the goods?
3   We can pay for the flat now so we don't have to worry about a bank loan.
4   Their business is quite small so they have to be careful with cashflow.
5   The software was available as a download so he didn't have to buy it on disc.
6   We'll have to order some photocopying paper. We're almost out of stock.

22

1 A: If we order 200 units, will you give us a 10 per cent discount?
   B: I'm afraid we can only offer 5 per cent on orders of that size.
2 C: We would expect you to cover insurance as well.
   D: Sorry but we can't agree to that. We can only cover freight.
3 A: We'd like you to deliver immediately.
   B: I'm sorry but that's not possible. We can only guarantee delivery within ten days.
4 A: We'll ship the goods by train. Is that all right?
   B: We'd rather you shipped them by road, in fact.
5 C: You'll have to pay us in advance this time.
   D: Well, we'd prefer to pay you on delivery as usual.

23

1 syllable: stopped; moved; watched
2 syllables: waited; reduced; offered
3 syllables: advertised; attracted; decided

24

1 receive; received
2 finance; financed
3 adapt; adapted
4 end; ended
5 launch; launched
6 count; counted
7 start; started

25

1 earn; earned
2 need; needed
3 describe; described
4 test; tested
5 discover; discovered
6 ask; asked
7 focus; focused
8 increase; increased
9 invest; invested
10 discuss; discussed

26

1 A: Were they trying to develop a new drug?
   B: Well, everybody thinks they were.
2 A: She was travelling around the world on her own.
   B: Are you sure she was?
3 A: Our competitors weren't promoting their range of products very well.
   B: Weren't they really?
4 A: The new product wasn't attracting a lot of customers.
   B: Well, in fact I think it was.
5 A: He was planning the next advertising campaign.
   B: Yeah and he was designing a new product at the same time.

27

Speaker 1: All right, then. It seems that we all agree when we should launch our new product so let's move on now to advertising.
Speaker 2: As you all know, the purpose of our meeting this afternoon is to decide how we're going to promote our new range.
Speaker 3: It's getting rather late, so let's sum up and see what we've got so far.
Speaker 4: Martin suggested that we should target supermarkets only. Helen, any thoughts on that?
Speaker 5: OK everyone? So the next item on our agenda is our R&D budget.
Speaker 6: Right. Quite a few suggestions have been made. So let's stop here for a minute and recap.
Speaker 7: So, you know what the problem is and you've heard a number of possible solutions. What are your views on this? Kim?
Speaker 8: I've called this meeting to exchange ideas about a new marketing strategy.

28

1 Right. Let's now have a look at our sales figures.
2 I'm not very happy about that, I'm afraid.
3 Just a minute, please.
4 Shall we get started?
5 Let's get down to business.
6 Well, I'm not sure about that.
7 What exactly do you mean by 'specialist stores'?
8 I'm in favour of launching the product just before summer.

29

Shall we begin? As you know, we're going to launch a major new product – a unique soft drink with low sugar and carbon dioxide content. I've called this meeting for two main reasons. Firstly, we still have to agree when exactly we should launch the product. Secondly, we need your ideas for a new name, as many of you are not satisfied with the name *Vitafruit*.
So, let's turn to the launch date. Sania, what do you think would be the best date?

30

1 pressure; problem; promotion
2 workload; lifestyle; deadline
3 contracts; asks; psychologists
4 He resigned three months ago.
5 It's a study about stress in the workplace.
6 She's planned lots of projects.

31

1 She's completely changed her lifestyle.
2 He hasn't seen a stress counsellor yet.
3 They've appointed a new management team.
4 They haven't introduced flexitime yet.

32

1 They've never made a presentation.
2 He's never travelled abroad.
3 They've gone on a training course.
4 She's been under a lot of stress.
5 He hasn't taken time off work this year.
6 We haven't finished our report.

33

1 They were overworked, weren't they?
2 She's been under stress recently, hasn't she?
3 They weren't feeling relaxed, were they?
4 You haven't missed the deadline, have you?
5 He resigned last week, didn't he?
6 She didn't come to work yesterday, did she?

34

a) B: How about introducing flexitime?
b) B: What about asking your boss to stop putting them up?
c) B: Shall we call a meeting to discuss the problem so we can look for ways of making them less strict?
d) B: We could make sure they don't have to work overtime more than once a week.
e) B: I think we should carry out a survey to find out how many people would go to a gym.
f) B: Well, I suggest you take it home with you and finish it over the weekend, then.
g) B: Why don't we hire someone part-time if he can't manage alone?

35

1 What about finishing earlier on Fridays?
2 Why don't we have individual interviews with each member of staff?
3 Have you thought of making working hours more flexible?
4 I think we should forbid smoking on all our premises.
5 Why don't we redecorate the staff restaurant to make it look more cheerful?
6 How about offering staff free yoga classes?
7 I suggest that we increase staff holidays from three to four weeks.
8 It might be a good idea to set up a counselling service.

36

1 crab; lamb; water; salmon
2 entertainment; vegetables; baked; steak
3 onion; broccoli; lobster; bottled
4 dessert; service; turkey; atmosphere
5 medium; sweet; veal; healthy
6 starter; salty; draught; charge

37

1 A: You've bought some chocolates. Who are they for?
   B: I bought them for you!
2 A: What's it made of?
   B: I think it's made of wood.
3 A: What are they looking at?
   B: I think they're looking at you!
4 A: Where was he from?
   B: They say he was from Iceland.
5 A: I wonder if this is the train to Brussels or from Brussels.
   B: Sorry, no idea!

38

1 She put off the meeting.
2 She put it off.
3 I looked up their address.
4 I looked it up.

39

1 Several extra visitors turned up.
2 They took up our invitation.
3 She took us out to an excellent restaurant.
4 Jim took part in an unusual event.
5 We should set up online sales as soon as we can.

40

1 A: David, have you met Elisa Vasconcelos?
   B: No. Hello, Elisa. Nice to meet you.
2 A: Jameel, do you know Sylvia?
   B: Yes, of course. Hi Sylvia, good to see you again.
3 A: How do you do? My name's Ralph Karsten.
   B: Nice to meet you. Mine's Brendan Lenihan.
4 A: How are things?
   B: Fine thanks. It's good to be here.
5 A: Can I get you something to drink?
   B: That would be nice, thanks. I'll have some fruit juice.

41

1 Did your flight get in on time?
2 How's your hotel?
3 Have you been here before?
4 Do you know your way around?
5 How long are you staying?
6 Could I use your phone, please?

42

1 I've just got off the train from Kyiv.
2 The food here is really delicious.
3 My daughter plays the piano as well.
4 I go to tai chi classes three times a week.
5 I'm in food quality control.
6 I worked in Malaysia for three years.
7 I'm from Gdansk.

43

not; nought
spot; sport
wok; walk

44

1 We'll send them all on a training course.
2 Let's sort out this problem before Pauline gets here.
3 According to this report, interest rates will soon fall.
4 We need to reform our tax system in order to stimulate exports.
5 They've closed forty of their stores and cut their workforce by a quarter.

45

1 the fifteenth of June
2 June fifteenth

46

1 the fourteenth of May
2 September fifteenth
3 the sixteenth of April
4 December seventeenth

47

1 the twentieth of February
2 February twentieth
3 the thirtieth of August two thousand and eight
4 July thirtieth, two thousand and ten
5 the twenty-third of May nineteen ninety
6 January thirteenth two thousand and three
7 the twelfth of October nineteen ninety-nine
8 the third of November

48

1 Thirteen pounds
2 Forty per cent
3 Three hundred and fifty million
4 One thousand, four hundred and sixteen yen
5 Eighty thousand dollars
6 One thousand, two hundred euros
7 Two-fifths
8 One point seven four

49

1 A: Did the unemployment rate decrease?
   B: Yes. It went down by 0.5 per cent to reach 7.9 per cent.
2 A: Do you know the Footsie index?
   B: Hold on … . Yes. It closed 114.2 points higher at 5,833.9 points.
3 A: What's the basic rate of income tax in the UK?
   B: Well, I guess it must be round about 20 per cent.
4 A: And what percentage of all income taxpayers pay the basic rate?
   B: About 75 or 80 per cent, I think.
5 A: What's the euro–dollar exchange rate?
   B: Mm, I'm not sure but I thought one euro was about 1.3 US dollars. Hold on, I'll check.
6 A: What's the population of the UK?
   B: Mm, just over 62 million, I'd say. So that's over 250 people per square kilometre.

50

And now in our business programme, here is *The Country in Figures*.
The growth rate of the economy last year was 3.1 per cent and the GDP per capita was $26,200.
The inflation rate was 2.3 per cent.
The labour force is estimated at 2.967 million; 81 per cent are employed in the services, 14 per cent in industry and 5 per cent in agriculture.
The unemployment rate fell to 4.9 per cent.
Finally, let's turn to the budget. Revenues totalled $54.7 billion and expenditure $53.1 billion.
With me in the studio is Professor Gary Myers of the National Institute of Economics. So Professor Myers, what are the prospects for the next six months?

51

1 A: Was that 2.5 per cent?
   B: No. 2.8 per cent.
2 A: Did you say 2.4 per cent?
   B: Sorry, no. 3.4 per cent.

52

1 A: So the unemployment rate went up by 1.2 per cent.
   B: Sorry, no, it was 1.1 per cent.
2 A: So, 36.7 per cent of the people in Denmark own a computer.
   B: 37.7 per cent, to be precise.
3 A: Did you say the GDP totalled £853 billion last year?
   B: Not quite. I said £843 billion.

53

available; place; marketing; advert; want; percentage

54

/ə/ as in about Canada: company; corporate
/æ/ as in bad bank: campaign; thanks
/eɪ/ as in play safe: behaviour; favourite
/ɪ/ as in quick fix: advantage; image
/ɑː/ as in smart card: forecast; target
/ɒ/ as in top job: quality; wasn't

55

1 Which age group *do you* belong to?
2 How much *did you* spend on soft drinks last month?
3 *Would you* consider buying a different brand?

56

1 Do you take the packaging into account?
2 How often do you buy spring water?
3 How many bottles of water did you buy last week?
4 Would you try fruit-flavoured mineral water?
5 What kind of soft drinks do you usually buy?

57

1 A: ... and your agent in Uruguay is Juan José Buaro. B-U-A-R-O ...
   B: Sorry, no. B-U-E-R-O.
2 A: All right. See you on Tuesday, then.
   B: Hold on a minute. The meeting is on Thursday.

58

1 A: Ah, hello Miss Peterson.
   B: Hello Mr Gallegos, it's Mrs Peterson, actually. How can I help you?
2 A: ... and my sales report will be with you by the thirtieth.
   B: Sorry, Ranesh. We're talking about the thirteenth.
3 A: So their number is 020 8224 7895.
   B: No, 8224 6895.
4 A: ... and you said the advertising agency was at 75 Birchington Street.
   B: Well, it's Birchington Road, actually.
5 A: I hear you increased your market share by 9.5 per cent.
   B: Sorry, I said 5.5 per cent.
6 A: And you said 40 per cent of the people you interviewed had difficulty finding our products.
   B: That's not quite right. I said 14 per cent.

59

1 A: We interviewed more than ***** people.
   B: Sorry, how many people did you interview?
2 A: ***** is unhappy about our sales figures.
   B: The line's very bad, I'm afraid. Who's unhappy about our sales figures?

60

1 A: So our new hair conditioner will be launched on *****.
   B: I couldn't hear you. When will it be launched?
2 A: We've already spent ***** on advertising.
   B: Sorry? How much have you spent?
3 A: The ***** Manager was really very pleased.
   B: Sorry, who was very pleased?
4 A: He'd like to meet you on ***** in the afternoon.
   B: It's a very bad line. When would he like to meet me?
5 A: Our new range of toiletries should be targeted at *****.
   B: Sorry? Who should our new range be targeted at?
6 A: Our total sales were over *****.
   B: Sorry, how much were they?

61

holiday; do; information; ordinary; other; overspend; work

62

/ɒ/ as in top job: holiday; office
/ɔː/ as in short course: ordinary; forecast
/uː/ as in school rules: do; move
/ʌ/ as in much luck: other; company
/ɜː/ as in first term: work; world
/ə/ as in about Canada: information; period
/əʊ/ as in go slow: overspend; open

63

1 They expect to make a huge profit.
2 They are going to relaunch the series very soon.
3 They are hoping to attract foreign investors.

64

1 What are you going to do?
2 They intend to expand in Poland.
3 He is planning to take early retirement.
4 We're hoping to open a subsidiary in Madrid.
5 They're going to do some research on their new product.

65

1 in**form**; infor**ma**tion
2 **imple**ment; implemen**ta**tion
3 pre**pare**; prepa**ra**tion
4 con**si**der; conside**ra**tion
5 **cele**brate; cele**bra**tion
6 **re**novate; reno**va**tion
7 ex**pand**; ex**pan**sion
8 ex**pect**; expec**ta**tion
9 **mo**dernise; moderni**sa**tion
10 dis**cuss**; dis**cu**ssion
11 de**cide**; de**ci**sion
12 re**vise**; re**vi**sion

66

Extract 1:
M: So after their meeting with the Marketing Manager, we'll take them to our research centre and …
F: Hold on a minute. What about lunch?
M: Sorry Ana. We agreed five minutes ago that lunch would be *after*, not *before* the visit to the centre.
Extract 2:
F: … and in about two weeks, we'll probably …
M: But we can't wait that long!
F: If you'll just let me finish, David, please. So what I was saying was …
Extract 3:
M: One thing is sure. We need to give our customers the opportunity to spread the cost of the products they wish to purchase.
F: How do you mean exactly?
Extract 4:
M: I don't think November is a good time to start the renovation. It's rather busy then, isn't it?
F: You mean, we do quite a lot of business then?
Extract 5:
F: … and another measure we've taken is to cancel the end-of-year party.
M: Erm, could I just comment on that?
F: Sorry Jimmy. I'll deal with comments and questions in a couple of minutes.
Extract 6:
M: As you can see from this graph, our sales figures …
F: Sorry, Bill. I think you've got the wrong slide on.

67

1 A: We forecast an increase in sales.
  B: Are you saying that business is picking up, then?
2 A: I don't think I can finish my report by Wednesday.
  B: So what you're saying is that you won't be able to meet the deadline.
3 A: Unfortunately, they didn't estimate the costs properly.
  B: You mean, it was a lot more expensive?
4 A: I hope Peterson will attend the board meeting.
  B: You mean, you are not completely sure he'll come?
5 A: They're not expecting to move into their new offices until January.
  B: So what you're saying is that they are not sticking to their plan.
6 A: It seems that there's going to be a slight delay.
  B: What exactly do you mean by 'slight delay'?

68

Kati: Szilvia?
Szilvia: Yes. Speaking.
Kati: Hi. I'm phoning about our visitors from Stockholm. I'm afraid they've changed their plans.
Szilvia: You mean, they're not coming next week?
Kati: Yes, they are. But they're arriving on Thursday, not on Wednesday as they originally planned.
Szilvia: I see. So what about our meeting?
Kati: Well, I think they're going to be very busy all day Thursday. You know, the performance evaluations and all that. They could see you after that but I'm sure Friday morning would be better. Would 10 o'clock be convenient for you?
Szilvia: Well, I'm seeing an important client at 10.15. I can't change that, I'm afraid.
Kati: How about earlier, say 8.30?
Szilvia: All right. Let's make it 8 o'clock, just to be on the safe side.
Kati: Fine. I'll confirm the appointment as soon as possible.
Szilvia: Thanks, Kati. That's great.

69

1 sales; training; persuasive; pay
2 launch; order; report; talk
3 money; number; other; trust
4 flow; approach; goal; shareholder

70

1 They told every one of us.
2 She finds it easy to delegate authority.
3 He believes in his employees' abilities.
4 They've invested a lot in training courses.
5 She likes to communicate information as often as possible.

71

1 He gained a lot of experience abroad.
2 She told us that Alan wouldn't agree.
3 The department isn't investing enough in training.

72

budget; invoice
mistake; support
shareholder; deputy; manager
suggestion; assistant; consultant

73

1 Keep in touch.
2 We'll be in touch soon.
3 Have a safe journey back.
4 I hope we'll see you again soon.
5 Thanks for looking after me so well.
6 Thanks ever so much for your hospitality.

74

1 A: What do you usually do after work?
  B: Not much. I sometimes watch a DVD.
2 A: Any plans for this evening?
  B: Well, I'd just like to stay in the hotel and relax.
3 A: What do people here usually do at weekends?
  B: Many people go to their holiday cottages in the hills.
4 A: We're going out. Why don't you join us?
  B: That's very kind of you but some other time.
5 A: How do you usually spend the summer?
  B: We all go to see my parents in Toulouse.
6 A: So what do you think of Copenhagen?
  B: It's great. Thanks for showing me around.

75

1   We're all sorry to see you leave.
2   It's been a pleasure working with you.
3   Goodbye. All the best.
4   Thanks very much for your hospitality.
5   Have a good weekend.

76

1   Hello. This is Max. I'm calling about your presentation on Friday. Just a couple of questions. What time would you like to start? And is the boardroom OK? Thanks. Bye.
2   Hi. Sue Short from Datatrax here. I'm phoning about your order number AB/987. We don't have Item 14 in stock, I'm afraid. Can we send you another model of the same quality?
3   Hi. This is Phil from Human Resources. I'm phoning about next week's job interviews. How many candidates do you want to interview? And something else: do you need any help?
4   Hello. Yeliz Gumus here. I'm ringing about your visit to Izmir. I've booked you into the Crowne Plaza Hotel. Could you send me your flight details, by the way? Thanks.

77

patient; nervous
propose; success
behaviour; consistent
compromise; sympathy

78

1   advice
2   solution
3   company
4   complaint
5   customer
6   entertainment

79

1   We won't pay.
2   We'll see.
3   We wouldn't answer.
4   We'd complain.
5   I'll do it.
6   I'd agree.
7   She'll send it.
8   She'd sign it.

80

1   I'd resign immediately.
2   I'll send them a fax.
3   We'll deliver the goods this week.
4   They'd close our account.
5   We wouldn't reduce the price.
6   We'd pay all transport costs.
7   They won't pay you a higher commission.
8   We won't sign the contract.

81

1   If we pay late, they'll close our account.
2   If you delivered this week, we'd pay all transport costs.
3   If you gave us a 10 per cent discount, we'd place our order early next week.
4   If you exceed the sales target, they'll give you a bonus.
5   If you pay cash, we'll give you an extra discount.

82

Speaker 1: ... so it was relatively easy to agree on transport and insurance but they wouldn't give us the usual 10 per cent discount. We told them 5 per cent was unacceptable. They wouldn't compromise so in the end we said we didn't want the goods and we turned to a new supplier.

Speaker 2: ... yeah, bosses come and go, don't they? The new one seems OK. At least she listens to us. That's what we need in sales – more than in any other department, I think. The one before was so inconsistent and unsympathetic, he just couldn't work with us. That's when three of our best representatives decided to leave the company.

Speaker 3: ... and he called me into his office on Tuesday morning and started shouting at me! Would you believe it? He said that I always handed in my reports late. Fortunately, I still had that e-mail he'd sent me, informing me he was expecting my report on Thursday afternoon. I showed it to him and in the end he did say he was sorry for being unfair. Good thing he did, otherwise I was prepared to resign.

Speaker 4: Every week I had four or five employees come up to me and complain about all the paperwork and about having to work much longer hours because of that. I knew they were right, there had been far too many redundancies. What could I do? I thought the best compromise was to hire some part-time administrative assistants and that's exactly what we did.

Speaker 5: We were working on the same project in three different teams, each working according to a different schedule. We were getting on well in my team – until Tony Debeer joined us, that is. We disagreed about almost everything and I found him very arrogant. We couldn't be more different, in fact. I found it all very stressful so I just said to our team leader that the schedule no longer suited me and I asked her to transfer me to another team.

83

A: Phillip's Office Supplies International. Good morning.
B: It's Mary Li here, from Sun Sing Advertising.
A: Hello, Ms Li. How can I help you?
B: I'd like to make a complaint.
A: What seems to be the trouble?
B: You have just sent us the wrong invoice, I'm afraid.
A: Can you give me the details, please.
B: Right. The invoice number is 202A and the order number you quote is BG/505. In fact, our order number is BG/503.
A: Now, let me see. I'm terribly sorry. It's our fault entirely. I'm afraid there's been a mix-up.
B: When do you think you can sort it out?
A: I'll look into it and call you back as soon as possible.
B: Thank you.
A: Don't mention it. Goodbye, Ms Li.

84

1   stylish; grow; produce
2   comfortable; manufacture
3   Our new products are attractive and practical.
4   They're also flexible and user-friendly.
5   It's designed for customers with busy lifestyles.
6   They haven't announced the launch date yet.

85

1   It's ideal for storing CDs.
2   It's got lots of interesting features.
3   Its weight is just under 3 kilos.
4   Its most attractive feature is that it's easy to operate.
5   It's got all you need for home and office use.
6   It's available in three different colours.

86

1   It's delivered within a week.
2   They're manufactured in Korea.
3   It was modified after the tests.
4   They were discontinued because of poor sales.
5   It's been advertised in all the national newspapers.
6   They've been promoted extensively.
7   It'll be tested in our laboratories.
8   They'll be insured against fire.

87

1   Could you tell us something about the special features of your office furniture?
2   What colours is it available in?
3   And what about the weight of this handheld TV?
4   Did you say it has an energy-saving device?
5   So what's its unique selling point?
6   What kind of guarantee do you offer?

88

Our new model has several special features which will appeal to our customers. It's stylish and it's made of stainless steel. It weighs just under 2.2 kilos and its length is 21 centimetres. It's ideal for the office. Another advantage is that it's very user-friendly. And finally, it costs 99 euros – great value for money!

89

Extract 1: ... and it comes in two elegant colours and gives you optimum efficiency while taking up a minimum of space. In just a few minutes, water is heated to the ideal temperature for a rich Italian taste. And a small heater built into the top will always keep your cups perfectly warm.
Extract 2: ... and it's got a timer, which makes it ideal for office or domestic use. It's 75cm high, 45cm wide and 30cm deep and weighs 40kg. It's ideal for room sizes of up to 25 square metres. Besides its incredible cooling facility, it also has a heating mode ...
Extract 3: It is designed for those who want hi-tech in their business and need high-quality colour documents. It can detect paper type and then select the ideal mode for any paper or film ...
Extract 4: It's the most exclusive model in our Eternity collection, designed for you to enjoy the art of precision timekeeping. It's got a steel casing, a pearl white dial and a large red second hand. It comes with a black natural rubber strap that has our logo in blue and white enamel on it ...
Extract 5: It is robust but not noticed easily. It uses PIR (Passive Infra Red) technology to detect body heat if somebody breaks in. And the whole system is controlled by a user-friendly keypad ...
Extract 6: Spacious and light, it is provided with a removable divider, key-operated locks and digital combination. Made from highly resistant cowhide leather, it includes a new innovative twisting handle ...